A DISSERTATION ON THE POOR LAWS

A DISSERTATION
ON THE POOR LAWS

BY A WELL-WISHER TO MANKIND

Joseph Townsend

FOREWORD BY ASHLEY MONTAGU

AFTERWORD BY MARK NEUMAN

UNIVERSITY OF CALIFORNIA PRESS

BERKELEY · LOS ANGELES · LONDON

1971

University of California Press
Berkeley and Los Angeles, California
University of California Press, Ltd.
London, England
Copyright © 1971, by The Regents of the University of California
ISBN: 0-520-01700-5
Library of Congress Catalog Card Number: 79-111419
Printed in the United States of America

CONTENTS

FOREWORD

BOOKS that have changed the human mind and transformed the world have, upon their appearance, usually made some noise. One thinks of Malthus's *Essay on the Principle of Population* (1798) and of Darwin's "Abstract," as he called it, *On the Origin of Species* (1859). Every educated person has, at least, heard of these two books, for their ideas have become a part of our culture and continue to reverberate to this day. They are books that are constantly being referred to in every possible connection, and their influence seems to increase rather than diminish with each syllable of recorded time. They are "seminal" books, that is, they are original and originative of new ideas having the most fructifying effects upon men's thought and conduct.

Occasionally a similar work, book, pamphlet or tract, is published, is widely read, debated, reprinted, and having made its mark, quietly fades away and is forgotten. Such a work is *A Dissertation on the Poor Laws. By a Well-Wisher to Mankind*, published at one shilling and sixpence at London in 1786. That this book has been so thoroughly forgotten is, from the viewpoint of the student of the history of ideas, not a little surprising, for it is to this extraordinary tract that both Malthus and Darwin owed the inspiration for their particular theories—the one more or less directly, and the other indirectly through his reading of Malthus in 1838.

The author of *A Dissertation* was Joseph Townsend, who was, at the time of the publication of this, his third tract, well known as a geologist, the great friend of William Smith, the Father of English geology, and rector of

Pewsey in Wiltshire. Shortly after Townsend's death the obituarist in the *Gentleman's Magazine* wrote of him that "as a scholar, a mineralogist, a fossilist, and conchologist, he stood pre-eminent," adding that Townsend's "extensive, exquisitely beautiful and scientifically arranged Collection of Minerals, and Organic Remains illustrative of the strata of the Earth and particularly of this island" was unique.[1]

Joseph Townsend was born in London, 4 April 1739, and died at Pewsey in Wiltshire, 9 November 1816. His father, Chauncey, was a respected merchant in Austin Friars, London, and his mother, Bridget, was a daughter of James Phipps, governor of Cape Coast Castle. His paternal uncle, James Townsend, was a well-known alderman of the city of London. Townsend took his B.A. at Clare Hall, Cambridge in 1762 and proceeded M.A. in 1765, when he was elected a Fellow of his college. He then studied medicine under Cullen in Edinburgh, practiced for some years as a physician, and finally settled for the Church. For a time his sympathies were strongly with the Calvinistic Methodists, during which period he occasionally preached in Lady Huntingdon's chapel at Bath. Following brief service as chaplain to the Duke of Atholl, Townsend became rector of Pewsey. During this period he fell under the lash of his neighbor Richard Graves (1715–1804), the rector of Claverton, near Bath. Graves, in his satire *The Spiritual Quixote* (1772), described, among others, Townsend's peculiarities and made sport with the views of the Methodists in general.[2] Townsend was twice married, first in 1773 to Joyce Neukivell of Truro, and after her death in 1875 he married, in 1780, Lydia Hammond, widow of Sir John Clerke. By his first wife Townsend had four sons and two daughters.

[1] Mr. Urban, *Gentleman's Magazine* 86, pt. 2 (November 1816): 606.
[2] Ibid.

In 1769, Townsend travelled in Ireland, and in subsequent years in France, Holland, and Flanders. Following these peregrinations he visited Spain and Switzerland. In whatever places he visited Townsend made careful note of the conditions of life of the people. His book, *A Journey Through Spain in the Years 1786 and 1787*, published in three volumes in 1791, and in new editions in 1792 and 1814, was widely read and admired. The book displays the wide range of Townsend's knowledge, and was justly described by the economic historian J. R. McCulloch as "one of the best works of the kind that has ever appeared, throwing a great deal of light upon the political economy of Spain, and on the causes of her decline."[3] It remains, indeed, an outstanding socioeconomic study of a complex society, a highly readable and engaging work.

A Journey Through Spain was a full-dress three-decker, and it remains Townsend's best-known work. *A Dissertation on the Poor Laws* was a small octavo of ninety-nine pages. It appears to have received a good deal of attention at the time of publication. A French translation was issued in 1800, and a new printing appeared a year after the author's death, in 1817, with an unsigned preface, which is known to be by William Wyndham, Baron Grenville. The preface is humane, critical, and admiring. An excerpt from it may be quoted.

The experience of thirty years has but too fatally verified our author's predictions. The mischiefs of the Poor Laws, such as he has described them, have ever since been increasing with an alarming rapidity. At the present moment everyone feels how much they aggravate the other difficulties of the country. But great as it is, this evil is not the greatest which these laws produce. They are still more pernicious in their moral than in their financial operation. They have already

[3] J. R. McCulloch, *The Literature of Political Economy* (London: Longman, Brown, Green and Longman's, 1845), p. 215.

done much to vitiate the habits, disposition, and character, of a very large portion of our people; and they have disordered the frame of our society itself, by weakening away its different parts, the mutual relations and feelings of benevolence and attachment.[4]

This view was widely shared by such diverse individuals as Burke, Pitt, Bentham, and Ricardo, not to mention numerous others.

Never were there a more important ninety-nine pages written than Townsend's *Dissertation*. It is because of that neglected fact and the originality of the views it expresses, views which so profoundly influenced the thinking of such men as Malthus, Darwin, and their contemporaries, that I have felt it desirable to bring this work to the attention of the reader interested in the history of ideas.

A *Dissertation* is a tract on political economy, a polemic on the Poor Laws, both existing and contemplated in Townsend's day. As we shall see, it is much more than that, and because it is so much more, it is difficult to understand the unmerited obscurity into which it has fallen. As a fascinating discussion of the inefficacy of the Poor Laws, Townsend's arguments possess a certain contemporary topicality. In our own day "relief" and talk of a guaranteed annual income constitute the modern equivalents of the debate which raged about the value of the Poor Laws during the latter quarter of the eighteenth century, and for many years thereafter. Almost two centuries have elapsed since Townsend's attack on the Poor Laws. He would have argued as vehemently against "relief," and he would undoubtedly have been utterly appalled by the idea of a guaranteed annual income. Yet, in spite of his *Dissertation*, he lived to see the Speenhamland plan instituted. This plan, resolved upon at a meeting of the

---

[4] A *Dissertation on the Poor Laws* (London: Ridgeways, 1817), p. vi.

justices of Berkshire, in Speenhamland, near Newbury, on 6 May 1795, was brought into being at a time of great distress. It recommended that subsidies in aid of wages should be granted in accordance with a scale dependent upon the price of bread, so that a minimum income should be guaranteed to the poor regardless of their earnings. This "right to live" measure continued as the law of the land over the greater part of the countryside till it was abolished 14 August 1834 by the passage of the New Poor Law which limited payment of charitable doles to sick and aged paupers and established workhouses where able-bodied paupers were put to work. Townsend had anticipated this policy and rejected it, dying a generation before it was enacted into law.

The Speenhamland plan represented the culmination of a long history of social legislation throughout Europe dating back to medieval times and even earlier. The appalling lot of the poor during this period has been many times described, but perhaps seldom more poignantly than by Lecky in his *History of European Morals*. In continental Europe the relief of the poor had been almost wholly in the hands of the ecclesiastical authorities. With the breakup of feudalism and, in England and Scotland, the Reformation and the dissolution of the monasteries, the state was forced to take over this responsibility. It was in this manner that poor laws came into being. From their institution until the present day there has never been a time when these laws were not under constant discussion.

In the Book of Books it is written that "the poor shall never cease out of the land" (Deuteronomy, 15:11), a station to which God had called them, just as he had called the rich man to his. This thought is engagingly expressed in a hymn that must have been sung by millions of English–speaking people, ending with the words:

> The rich man in his castle
> The poor man at his gate,
> God made them, high or lowly,
> And ordered their estate.[5]

Such ideas were the common currency of the descendants of Calvinistic individualism, with its doctrine of the elect and the non-elect, and of the Puritans, with their belief in wealth as an evidence of divine grace, and poverty as a sign of moral error. For both Calvinists and Puritans, and for the creators of the Protestant ethic, it was all a matter of predestination. God's word in these matters was sufficient for the sixteenth and seventeenth centuries. In the eighteenth century God's word was reinforced by Natural Law and often identified with it: God expressed himself through nature's laws. It is no accident that Darwin's forerunners, Townsend and Malthus, should have been churchmen with natural-science interests, and that Darwin, who had originally been intended for the Church, should, in the nineteenth century, have taken the view that God and nature's laws expressed themselves most efficiently through the intelligence of the student of nature.

Writers such as Francis Bacon, Sir Walter Raleigh, Thomas Hobbes, John Graunt, William Petty, Adam Smith, Benjamin Franklin, David Hume, Sir James Steuart, Montesquieu, Condorcet, Arthur Young, and most notably Robert Wallace, had all written interestingly on the subject of population pressures and their consequences, anticipating in many respects the views later developed by Townsend and Malthus. It was, however, the American Revolution and the writings of the philosophes which brought things to a head. Almost certainly the rise of the antislavery movement also played a part in this social ferment which later led, among other things, to the

---

[5] By Cecil Alexander (1818–1895).

production of such works in England as William God-win's *Political Justice* (1793), the treatise to which Malthus's *Essay* was the direct rejoinder.

In France the second half of the eighteenth century saw the rise of the physiocrats, les économistes, led by François Quesnay (1694–1774), court physician to Louis XV and Madame de Pompadour. The physiocrats as economists saw the business of getting and spending as *ex natura jus*, a matter of the government of nature. It was a biological model that inspired the physiocratic theory of the organic self-perpetuating nature of life in economic society. As a physician and surgeon Quesnay was much excited by Harvey's demonstration of the circulation of the blood, and so, by analogy, he reasoned that just as the blood circulates through the body, nourishing its tissues and organs, yielding some of its ingredients and taking up others, returning to the lungs and heart to be replenished, so the wealth of society is replenished through production, exchange, and distribution in a strictly natural, harmonious manner. Economics, then, represented the physiology of economic society. It was, indeed, a natural science.[6] The setting in which economic laws work is natural, and its foundation is agriculture, for agriculture is the sole source of wealth. The poor are necessary to cooperate with nature in making its wealth available, by extracting it from the soil so that it can then be converted into consumable form.

Townsend was widely read in this literature, and it was in the agitative atmosphere to which these writings had contributed that Townsend produced his *Dissertation*. He wrote as a social philosopher who considered the Poor Laws inimical to the welfare of mankind, of which he was the professed well-wisher, and of society, of which he was a distinguished member. Townsend was himself a mem-

[6] François Quesnay, *Tableau Économique* (Versailles, 1758); also Quesnay's earlier work, *Essai Physique sur l'Économie Animale* (Paris, 1736).

ber of the rentier class, a fact which was not uninfluential in determining the character of his thinking on the Poor Laws. Our principal concern here, however, is not with Townsend's influence upon social legislation as such, but with his influence upon biological and social thinking, as expressed chiefly through the writings of Malthus and Darwin. To the discussion of this we may now proceed.

"The poor," writes Townsend, "know little of the motives which stimulate the higher ranks to action—pride, honour, and ambition. In general it is only hunger which can spur and goad them on to labour" (p. 23). "He who statedly employs the poor in useful labour, is their only friend; he, who only feeds them, is their greatest enemy" (p. 26). "Hunger will tame the fiercest animals, it will teach decency and civility, obedience and subjection, to the most brutish, the most obstinate, and the most perverse" (p. 27). That hunger is the balance-wheel maintaining the equilibrium of society, is Townsend's constant and consistently reiterated theme. This is interesting, but not in itself remarkable, were it not for the fact that Townsend makes this principle a law of nature and of society. "It seems to be a law of nature," he writes, "that the poor should be to a certain degree improvident, that there may always be some to fulfil the most servile, the most sordid, and the most ignoble offices in the community" (p. 35; also see p. 36).

Townsend's view of social stratification and the natural laws of class hierarchy and social obligation are at least as old as Aristotle. That the poor are naturally improvident may be a novel idea, but the fundamental theorem of the *Dissertation* (Sect. VIII) is arrived at after Townsend makes it quite clear that "in the very nature and constitution of the world" the Poor Laws must fail. To illustrate his point Townsend recounts the story of what is purported to have happened on Robinson Crusoe's island, Juan Fernández, off the coast of Chile. A few goats had been placed on the island by the Spanish admiral after whom the island had been named, Juan Fernández (c. 1536–1602?). These had increased at a biblical rate, providing a convenient supply of food for the British privateers and others who were molesting the Spanish ships. By introducing a greyhound dog and a bitch on the island the Spaniards hoped in a short time to reduce their enemies by cutting off their food supply. The dogs, so the story goes, multiplied and greatly diminished the number of goats. "Had they been totally destroyed," writes Townsend, "the dogs likewise must have perished. But as many of the goats retired to the craggy rocks, where the dogs could never follow them, descending only for short intervals to feed with fear and circumspection in the vallies, few of these, besides the careless and the rash, became a prey; and none but the most watchful, strong and active of the dogs could get a sufficiency of food. Thus a new kind of balance was established. The weakest of both species were among the first to pay the debt of nature; the most active and vigorous preserved their lives. It is the quantity of food which regulates the number of the human species" (p. 38).

In this passage written twenty-three years before Darwin's birth, and seventy-three years before the publication of Darwin's *Origin of Species*, the principle of natural selection is succinctly stated. This, also, is essentially the doctrine of Malthus expressed earlier and more clearly by Townsend. Darwin's statement of the principle of natural selection is as follows:

As many more individuals of each species are born than can possibly survive; and as, consequently, there is a frequently recurring struggle for existence, it follows that any being, if it vary however slightly in any manner profitable to itself, under the complex and sometimes varying conditions of life, will have a better chance of surviving, and thus be *naturally selected*. From the strong principle of inheritance, any selected variety will tend to propagate its new and modified form. [Or more specifically] . . . as more individuals are produced than can possibly survive, there must in every case be a struggle for existence, either one individual with another of the same species, or with the individuals of distinct species, or with the physical conditions of life. It is the doctrine of Malthus applied with manifold force to the whole animal and vegetable kingdoms.[7]

Malthus does not appear to have read the *Dissertation* before writing his *Essay*. In the preface to the second edition (1803) he states that further inquiry into the subject revealed that much more had been done than he had been aware of, and he names Townsend, among others, as one who had treated of the same subject in a like manner, expressing "a natural surprise that it had not excited more of the public attention."

But Townsend's work had not failed to excite "public attention." Malthus's father, Daniel—friend and host to Voltaire—almost certainly knew of it, the whole subject, as we have seen, having been in more or less continuous debate throughout the last fifteen years of the eighteenth century. While at his first writing Malthus may not have been familiar with the actual *Dissertation*, he could scarcely have escaped the views which, as Malthus later said, Townsend treated with such "great skill and perspicuity." Indeed, Karl Marx considered that the *Essay* was no more than "a schoolboyish, superficial plagiary of Defoe, Sir James Steuart, Townsend, Franklin, Wallace, &c., and does not contain a single sentence thought out by himself."[8] This harsh judgment need not be taken too

[7] Charles Darwin, *On the Origin of Species by Means of Natural Selection, or the Preservation of Favoured Races in the Struggle for Life* (London: John Murray, 1859), pp. 5, 63.
[8] Footnote to *Capital*, vol. 1, quoted in R. L. Meek, ed., *Marx and Engels on Malthus*, trans. D. and R. Meek (London: Lawrence and Wishart, 1953), p. 83.

seriously, but it does support the view that Malthus was
not writing in a vacuum, that Marx was fully aware of the
fact, if Malthus was not, that his ideas were not entirely
underived from other sources. If Malthus, as Karl Pearson
has said, was a strewer of seed which reached its harvest in
Charles Darwin and others, it is equally true that Townsend was a strewer of seed which fructified in the fertile
brain of Thomas Robert Malthus. As one of the few
writers of our own day acquainted with the importance of
the Townsendian ideas has put it in one of the most distinguished works of its kind, "Neither Darwin's theory of
natural selection, nor Malthus' population laws might
have exerted any appreciable influence on modern society
but for the . . . maxims which Townsend deduced from
his goats and dogs and wished to have applied to the reform of the Poor Law."[9]

Darwin seems to have been completely unaware of
Townsend's *Dissertation*, but its influence upon him
through the medium of Malthus's *Essay* was decisive. It
is to be noted that both Townsend and Malthus were
writing as socio-political thinkers and not as natural
scientists or biologists. It is to such socio-political thinkers
that Darwin owed his explanation of the mechanism of
evolution.[10] As a member of the same social class to which
Townsend and Malthus belonged, he saw the great differ-
ences that existed between the classes much as these two
thinkers did. The struggle for existence among men was
paralleled by the struggle for existence among plants and
animals. It was not that the struggle among men was seen
as a part of the competition inherent in nature, but rather
that nature was seen as mirroring the struggle for existence of men living, or attempting to live, in a ruthless

[9] Karl Polanyi, *The Great Transformation* (New York: Rinehart & Co.,
1944), p. 113.
[10] Ashley Montagu, *Darwin, Competition, and Cooperation* (New York:
Henry Schuman, 1952).

industrial society in which the "fittest" alone survived. The "fittest" inherited what it took to survive, and by safeguarding and augmenting what they had, the favored classes were preserved in the struggle for existence, whereas those who inherited no property and were forced to work for a living would leave nothing to transmit to their progeny but their sins. It is written that "Unto everyone that hath shall be given, and he shall have abundance: but from him that hath not shall be taken away even that which he hath" (Matthew 25:29). If wealth was an evidence of election, and poverty a this-wordly sign that the Lord had turned his countenance away, Natural Law could not say otherwise. And this is precisely what Townsend demonstrated.

As Geddes pointed out as long ago as 1882, "The place vacated by Paley's theological and metaphysical explanation has simply been occupied by that suggested to Darwin and Wallace by Malthus in terms of the prevalent severity of industrial competition, and these phenomena of the struggle for existence which the light of contemporary economic theory has enabled us to discern, have thus come to be temporarily exalted into a complete explanation of organic progress."[11] The same interpretation was offered by that equally extraordinary genius, Charles S. Peirce, the founder of pragmatism, in a brilliant essay published in January 1893. Wrote Peirce, "*The Origin of Species* of Darwin merely extends politico–economical views of progress to the entire realm of animal and vegetable life."[12]

It is generally assumed that social thought after 1859 largely represented the reflection of Darwin's biology. The truth is that Darwinian biology was largely in-

---

[11] Patrick Geddes, *Chambers Encyclopaedia* (Edinburgh & London: A. & C. Black, 1882), s.v. "Biology."
[12] Charles S. Peirce, "Evolutionary Love," *Monist* 3 (January 1893): 176–200.

fluenced by the social, economic, and political thought of the first half of the nineteenth century, and that its own influence took the form of giving scientific support in the form of natural law for what had hitherto been factitiously imposed social law. Darwin provided the nineteenth century with a biological philosophy for industrial progress. This biological philosophy was based on the biological model provided by Joseph Townsend in his *Dissertation*, not, as I have already said, directly but indirectly through the agency of Malthus.

What Townsend did was to introduce, for the first time in the history of social thought, a biological model as a basis for the socioeconomic conduct of society, a putative "Natural Law," to guide the behavior of the classes in relation to one another. It is in this contribution, and in the influence it has exerted upon later social, political, and biological thought, that the importance of Townsend's *Dissertation* lies.

Princeton, New Jersey   ASHLEY MONTAGU
28 August 1970

THE WRITINGS OF
JOSEPH TOWNSEND

Every True Christian a New Creature. London, 1765.

Free Thoughts on Despotic and Free Governments. London, 1781.

The Physicians Vade-Mecum; or a concise system of the practice of physic. London, 1781.

A Dissertation on the Poor Laws. London, 1786; 1787; 1817.

Observations on Various Plans Offered to the Public for the Relief of the Poor. London, 1788.

A Journey Through Spain in the Years 1786 and 1787 with particular attention to the agriculture, manufactures, commerce, population, taxes and revenue of that country, and remarks in passing through a part of France. 3 vols. London, 1791.

A Guide to Health; being cautions and directions in the treatment of diseases. 2 vols. 3d ed. London, 1795; 1796.

Elements of Therapeutics: or, A Guide to Health. 3d ed. London, 1801.

Sermons on Various Subjects. London, 1805.

The Character of Moses Established for Veracity as an Historian, Recording Events from the Creation to the Deluge. 2 vols. Bath, 1813–1815.

Etymological Researches, wherein numerous languages apparently discordant have their affinity traced and their resemblance so manifest as to lead to the conclusion that all languages are radically one, etc. London, 1824.

A DISSERTATION ON THE POOR LAWS

SECT. I

TO a man of common sensibility nothing can be more distressing, than to hear the complaints of wretchedness, which he hath no power to redress, and to be daily conversant with misery, which he can neither fly from, nor relieve. This at present is the situation of the clergy, who, in virtue of their office, are obliged to visit the habitations of the poor. Here they see helpless infancy and decrepit age, the widow and the orphan, some requiring food, and others physic; all in such numbers, that no private fortune can supply their wants. Such scenes are more distressing, when, as it sometimes happens, the suffering objects have been distinguished for industry, honesty, and sobriety. The laws indeed have made provision for their relief, and the contributions are more than liberal which are collected for their support; but then, the laws being inadequate to the purposes for which they were designed, and the money collected being universally misapplied, the provision, which was originally made for industry in distress, does little more than give encouragement to idleness and vice. The laws themselves appear beautiful on paper, and will be the admiration of succeeding ages, when, in the revolution of empires, the whole fabric of our government shall be dissolved, and our nation, as a separate kingdom, shall exist no more. These laws, so beautiful in theory, promote the evils they mean to remedy, and aggravate the distress they were intended to relieve. Till the reign of Q. Elizabeth they were unknown in England; and to the present moment, they have never been adopted by any other kingdom upon earth. It has been most unfortunate for us, that two of the greatest blessings have been productive of the greatest evils. The Revolution gave birth to that enormous load of debt, under which this nation groans; and to the Reformation we are indebted for the laws which multiply the poor.

At the dissolution of the monasteries, the lazy and the indigent, who were deprived of their accustomed food, became clamorous, and, having long since forgot to work, were not only ready to join in every scheme for the disturbance of the state, but, as vagrants, by their numbers, by their impostures, and by their thefts, they rendered themselves a public and most intolerable nuisance. To stop their mouths, and to make them employ their hands in honest labour, was the intention of that day. But at the same time the laws took under their protection some objects of distress, who for near two hundred years, from a noble kind of pride, refused the proffered aid, or received it with reluctance; and who at the present moment would be more effectually relieved, if no other laws existed but the first great laws of human nature, filial affection, and the general benevolence of mankind. The world, it must be confessed, is wicked enough: Yet amidst all their wickedness men seldom want compassion, unless the circumstances in which they find themselves are peculiarly distressing. Should we "in the straitness of a siege behold men eating the flesh of their sons and of their daughters; should we see among them a man tender and delicate, whose eye should be evil towards his brother and towards the wife of his bosom, and towards the remnant of his children, so that he should not give to any of them of the flesh of his children whom he should eat*;" we must not from such instances conclude that all men, or even most men, are destitute of mercy and compassion, or that man in general can be kind and beneficent only by compulsion. No doubt in every district will be found some, who are strangers to the finer feelings of the human heart; but at

* Deut. xxviii. 52.

the same time in every district will be found some, who are endued with generosity of soul; and others, who under the influence of piety will rejoice to relieve the wants and distresses of their fellow creatures. In every place some will be distinguished for benevolence, others for brutality; but in general man is what his situation makes him. Is he happy himself in the enjoyment of ease and affluence? In such circumstances "he will be eyes to the blind and feet to the lame; he will be a father to the poor; the blessing of those that are ready to perish will come upon this man: he will cause the widow's heart to leap for joy*." Let the same man be straitened in his circumstances, let him be burthened with taxes, let him be harassed by the clamours and distracted by the incessant demands of the most improvident and lazy of the surrounding poor; and he will have little inclination to seek for objects of distress, or to visit the sequestered cottage of the silent sufferer. It is generally found, that modest worth stands at a distance, or draws nigh with faltering tongue and broken accents to tell an artless tale; whilst the most worthless are the most unreasonable in their expectations, and the most importunate in their solicitation for relief. If the latter, from any imperfection of our laws, get abundantly too much, the former must of necessity obtain too little. If, agreeable to the general practice of the labouring poor, a man, previous to his marriage, or whilst his family is small, has made no provision for his future wants; if all, to whom he might naturally look for aid, are in the same circumstances with himself; and if the charity of those among his neighbours, who are distinguished for benevolence, nay of all who have the common feelings of humanity, is exhausted; if they who are most willing are least able to relieve him; we must expect to see distress and poverty even among those who are worthy of compassion. —This at present is the case in England. There never was

* Job, xxix.

greater distress among the poor: there never was more money collected for their relief. But what is most perplexing is, that poverty and wretchedness have increased in exact proportion to the efforts which have been made for the comfortable subsistence of the poor; and that wherever most is expended for their support, there objects of distress are most abundant; whilst in those countries or provincial districts where the least provision has been made for their supply, we hear the fewest groans. Among the former we see drunkenness and idleness cloathed in rags; among the latter we hear the chearful songs of industry and virtue.

If laws alone could make a nation happy, ours would be the happiest nation upon earth: idleness and vice could not exist; poverty would be unknown; we should be like a prosperous hive of bees; all would have enough and none too much. The reverse of this we find to be the case: poverty and vice prevail, and the most vicious have access to the common stock. If a man has squandered the inheritance of his fathers; if by his improvidence, by his prodigality, by his drunkenness and vices, he has dissipated all his substance; if by his debaucheries he has ruined his constitution, and reduced himself to such a deplorable condition that he hath neither inclination nor ability to work; yet must he be maintained by the sweat and labour of the sober and of the industrious farmer, and eat the bread which should be given only to virtue in distress.—If in all cases, this bread, so ill bestowed, were superabundant; if the industrious farmer were himself in ease and affluence; the grievance would yet be tolerable.— But in this day it often happens that the industrious farmer is oprest with poverty. He rises early, and it is late before he can retire to his rest; he works hard and fares hard; yet with all his labour and his care he can scarce provide subsistence for his numerous family. He would feed them better, but the prodigal must *first* be fed. He would purchase warmer cloathing for them, but the children of the prostitute must *first* be cloathed. The little which remains after the profligate have been cloathed and fed, is all that he can give to those, who in nature have the first claims upon a father. If this evil could be stemmed, whilst the present laws subsist, he might yet have hope: but when he considers, that all the efforts, which have been made in his own parish or in others, have been vain, and that the evil is constantly increasing, he is driven to despair of help, and fears that he shall be himself reduced to work for daily hire. It will be evident that his fears are not altogether groundless, if we consider, that even in parishes, where no manufactures have been established, the poor rates have been doubling, some every fourteen years, and others nearly every seven years; whilst in some districts, where the manufactures are carried on to a considerable extent, the poor rates are more than ten shillings in the pound upon the improved rents. That the distress does not arise from the high price of corn, will be clear, if we consider, what may perhaps hereafter be more fully stated, that although for these two hundred years the price of wheat has fluctuated between wide extremes, yet upon comparing the average prices within that period, the ancients did not find a cheaper market than the moderns. If we take the average of the sixty years which terminated at the commencement of the present century, we shall find the price of wheat to have been six shillings and four pence halfpenny per bushel, whereas in the subsequent sixty years it was only five shillings; and for the last twenty years, ending with the year 1782, not more than six shillings and six pence: yet during that long period in which provisions were the cheapest, the poor rates were continually advancing. That the distress does not arise from the high price of soap, leather, candles, salt, and other small articles needful in a family, will appear not only from the superior advance in the price of labour (in the proportion of six to four within a century)*, but from hence, that where the price of labour is the highest and provisions are the cheapest, there the poor rates have been most exorbitant. In Scotland they have no legal provision for the poor, yet labour is cheaper and corn is dearer than they are in England.

SECT. II

UNDER the best administration, the laws relating to the poor give occasion to much injustice; under the worst, they are too often the instruments of oppression and revenge. If the intentions of the magistrate are good, his compassion may be ill directed; but if at any time his judgment is blinded by his passions, in the keeness of his resentment for some real or imaginary affront, he is apt to forget the purpose for which the administration of the poor laws was committed to his care, and to abuse his power, by granting, when the property of his own tenants is not to be affected by it, the most ample relief to the most unworthy objects. This indeed would seldom happen, if none but gentlemen of a liberal education were put into the commission of the peace; or if, aggreeable to the original constitution of our government, this office were elective. But should the wisest and the best of men be chosen, yet we could not expect that such would every where be found willing to devote their time and whole attention to the administration of those laws, whose natural tendency is to increase the number of the poor, and greatly to extend the bounds of human misery.

* Sir William Petty, P. Arithmetic.

SECT. III

ALL who are conversant with Tacitus have admired the extent of his knowledge, the shrewdness of his remarks, and the nervous strength of his expression. In a speech which he puts into the mouth of the Roman emperor Tiberius, we find this passage: "Languescet industria, intendetur socordia, si nullus ex se metus aut specs, & securi omnes aliena subsidia expectabunt, sibi ignavi, nobis graves*." Hope and fear are the springs of industry. It is the part of a good politician to strengthen these: but our laws weaken the one and destroy the other. For what encouragement have the poor to be industrious and frugal, when they know for certain, that should they increase their store it will be devoured by the drones†? or what cause have they to fear, when they are assured, that if by their indolence and extravagance, by their drunkenness and vices, they should be reduced to want, they shall be abundantly supplied, not only with food and raiment, but with their accustomed luxuries, at the expence of others. The poor know little of the motives which stimulate the higher ranks to action—pride, honour, and ambition. In general it is only hunger which can spur and goad them on to labour; yet our laws have said, they shall never hunger. The laws, it must be confessed, have likewise said that they shall be compelled to work. But then legal constraint is attended with too much trouble, violence, and noise; creates ill will, and never can be productive of good and acceptable service: whereas hunger is not only a peaceable, silent, unremitted pressure, but, as the most

* L. ii. p. 73, 74. edit. Elf.
† Hesiod, 302.

natural motive to industry and labour, it calls forth the most powerful exertions; and, when satisfied by the free bounty of another, lays a lasting and sure foundation for good will and gratitude. The slave must be compelled to work; but the freeman should be left to his own judgment and discretion; should be protected in the full enjoyment of his own, be it much or little; and punished when he invades his neighbour's property. By recurring to those base motives which influence the slave, and trusting only to compulsion, all the benefits of free service, both to the servant and to the master, must be lost.

It is universally found, that where bread can be obtained without care or labour, it leads through idleness and vice to poverty. Before they discovered the gold and silver mines of Peru and Mexico, the Spaniards were distinguished among the nations of Europe for their industry and arts, for their manufactures and their commerce. But what are they now? a lazy, poor, and miserable people. They have been ruined by their imaginary wealth. The declension of the Spaniards has been attributed to the expulsion of the Moriscoes; and the blow was certainly severe, but not altogether adequate to the effect. The number expelled was more than six hundred thousand, besides those who died by the sword, by famine, or by the sentences of The Inquisition. The principal charge brought against them was their obstinate adherence to the Mahometan religion: the political reason assigned for their expulsion was, that by their industry, temperance, and frugality, they were able to work cheaper than the Spaniards, whilst by their sobriety they contributed little to the public revenue: but the real cause of this impolitic measure was an order from the Pope, that these infidels should be converted at the expence of the Spanish clergy. The Archbishop of Valentia was to pay three thousand six hundred ducats yearly, and the other bishops in proportion to their incomes, for the support of an Arabic mission*. Thus the temperate, the frugal, and the industrious, being banished from the kingdom, whilst the indolent found a constant influx of gold and silver from abroad, the whole nation sunk by degrees into the present state of torpid inactivity. It is more than one hundred and seventy years since this event, and yet in all that time Spain has not recovered her population. The quantity of gold and silver imported annually into Cadiz and Lisbon has been reckoned six millions sterling†. Here we find a sufficient cause for the decay of their industry and arts.

Our poor began only to appear in numbers after the dissolution of the monasteries. Then it was they first attracted notice; but they had existed long before, always most abundant in the vicinity of the religious houses. At the present moment we are told, that in Naples six thousand Lazaroni are daily fed by the monastic orders, under the specious name of charity, not upon a sudden emergency, but statedly, and as the only means of their subsistence. As a peace offering this may be politic and wise, well calculated to conciliate the good opinion of the unthinking mind, and to command the admiration of the vulgar; but at the same time it is inconsistent with the most established principles of political economy: for as industry and frugality are the only foundation of national prosperity; so temperance and labour are the only source of happiness and wealth to individuals. A learned Jesuit, who has lately written and is now publishing an elegant defence of that society, assumes great merit from this circumstance, that instead of extorting for themselves a scanty pittance from the vitals of the people, such was the benevolence of these holy fathers, and such the abundant wealth of their establishments, that they re-

* Geddes, Account of the Moriscoes.
† Smith, Wealth of Nations.

lieved all in the surrounding villages, who made application to their charity. Their intentions, no doubt, were good, but their bounty must have been misapplied. He, who statedly employs the poor in useful labour, is their only friend; he, who only feeds them, is their greatest enemy. Their hopes and fears should centre in themselves: they should have no hope but from their own sobriety, diligence, fidelity, and from the well-earnt friendship of their employers; and then their only fear would be the fear of forfeiting by their misconduct, that favour and protection which would be their principal resource in times of sickness and distress.

SECT. IV

A WISE legislator will endeavour to confirm the natural bonds of society, and give vigour to the first principles on which political union must depend. He will preserve the distinctions which exist in nature independent of his authority, and the various relations which, antecedent to his creation, connected man to man. He will study the natural obligations which arise from these relations, that he may strengthen these connections by the sanction of his laws. Among the first of these relations stands the relation of a servant to his master; and the first duty required from a servant is prompt, chearful, and hearty obedience. On this condition alone can the connection be preserved, as without due subordination all government must end. But our laws tend to weaken these bonds, and to destroy this subordination, by compelling the occupier of land to find employment for the poor. With this provision, what have they to fear when discharged from service? If one will not employ them, another must. If the work be slighted or neglected, if it be deserted in the pressing hour, or spoiled in the execution, it is to little purpose for the master to complain; he can have no redress. Does he seek relief from the civil power? The unequal contest is begun, and the remedy will be worse than the disease. Both the servant and the master know when the work is ill performed, or when the servant has not earnt his wages, even when legal proof is wanting. If then the master has no other remedy, he is at the mercy of his servants; he must connive at their neglects, and bear their impertinence with patience. There is no alternative but this, or to maintain them without work. The appeal in this case to a magistrate is from a superior tribunal to the inferior, from the stronger to the weaker. Where the natural sanctions are sufficient to secure obedience without disturbing the peace and good order of society; there a wise legislator will be careful not to interfere, lest, by weakening these, without being able to substitute better in their place, he should stop the course of justice and protect the guilty. The wisest legislator will never be able to devise a more equitable, a more effectual, or in any respect a more suitable punishment, than hunger is for a disobedient servant. Hunger will tame the fiercest animals, it will teach decency and civility, obedience and subjection, to the most brutish, the most obstinate, and the most perverse. A good servant need not be afraid of wanting work. If one master should dismiss him from his service, others will be happy to receive him. But should a man be notorious for a thief, and for spoiling or neglecting work; should he be either so false, so vicious, or so ill-tempered, that no master would be willing to employ him; it would certainly be just that he should suffer hunger till he had learnt to reform his conduct. There are perhaps few parishes which cannot produce some of this untoward disposition. Indeed it is the general complaint of farmers, that their men do not work so well as they used to do, when it was reproachful to be relieved by the parish.

SECT. V

IT may seem strange in a country where agriculture, arts, manufactures, and commerce, are most flourishing, all of which have a mutual and corresponding influence on each other, to say that the laws discourage manufactures; yet this may be said of the poor laws in England. By our present system we prevent their introduction, check their progress, and hasten their departure. If the rental of a parish were not bound to provide for the increasing poor, every gentleman of landed property would be solicitous to have manufacturers established on his estates, in order to consume the produce of his lands. By multiplying the consumers he would enhance the value of all the various products of the soil: he would enjoy the monopoly of hay and pasture, and share with all his neighbours to a given distance in the sale of corn. But when he considers that manufactures fluctuate, that the benefit which he is to derive from them will not bear proportion to the burthen which he must entail upon his property; he will rather wish to keep them at a convenient distance. The principal benefit he can expect is, that the value of his pastures should be doubled: but even whilst the manufacture prospers, the demands of the poor, both upon his arable and pasture, will be more than doubled, and when it fails, the poor's rate will swallow up the whole. The surrounding parishes will reap the chief advantage: he will have the happiness to see them flourish; but the load and burthen of the poor will remain upon his own estate. "Sic vos non vobis fertis aratra, boves*."

In every parish, as the law now stands, they who have legal settlements, have the monopoly of labour, because the labouring poor are confined to their respective parishes. This provision is perfectly consistent with the whole system of our poor laws, and was designed not only to prevent the evils which naturally arise from vagrancy, and which might be equally prevented by more wholesome laws; but to protect each parish from intruders, who might become chargeable either for themselves or for their children. This provision is productive of considerable evils, which the legislature has never yet been able to remove: for not only have the industrious poor been restrained from seeking employment where they would otherwise have been received with joy, and confined to their own parishes, in which they were regarded with an evil eye; but for want of competition the price of labour to the manufacturer has been much enhanced. With a certificate, indeed, the poor are permitted to reside in any parish where work is to be had, but then a certificate is not easily obtained. Now it is evident that by raising the price of labour you must directly check the progress of the manufactures; and by experience it is found, that the same effect arises indirectly to a more considerable extent; for in proportion as you advance the wages of the poor, you diminish the quantity of their work. All manufacturers complain of this, and universally agree, that the poor are seldom diligent, except when labour is cheap, and corn is dear. It must be confessed that too many of them have some little resemblance to the animal described by travellers under the name of Nimble Peter; a creature so inactive, that, when he has cleared one tree, he will be reduced to skin and bones before he climbs another, and

* Virgil's Complaint.

so slow in all his motions, that even stripes will not make him mend his pace*. Drunkenness is the common vice of poverty; not perhaps of poverty as such, but of the uncultivated mind; for it is the characteristic of unpolished nations to be fond of intoxicating liquors. Whatever be the cause, it is notorious, that with the common people the appetite for strong drink is their prevailing appetite. When therefore, by the advance in wages, they obtain more than is sufficient for their bare subsistence, they spend the surplus at the alehouse, and neglect their business. Is a man drunk one day? He will have little inclination to work the next. Thus for every drunken fit two days are lost. By frequent repetition the habit is confirmed, and, by reducing the number of working days, their value is enhanced. In proportion to this loss, the price of labour will be raised. As long as men have nothing to fear, either for themselves or for their families, this practice will prevail. Where the price of labour is advanced, the industrious and the sober will by degrees acquire a taste for luxury. They will not be contented with bare subsistence, with a sufficient quantity of coarse yet wholesome food, with warm but homespun garments, and with healthy but unfurnished cottages: they will contract habits of refinement, which, when suffered to promote their industry, will be useful both to themselves and to the public, but which in all cases, will have a tendency to keep up the price of labour, and to advance the price of all those articles which they consume. Even they who do not work must eat, and, by increasing the demand for corn, will enhance its value, and consequently the price of labour. In this case action and re-action are equal, but not opposite. The high price of labour raises the value of provisions, and the high price of provisions enhances the value of labour. They are both increased by the present system of our poor laws, and have both a tendency to check the

* Dampier, Vol. ii. Part ii. p. 61.

progress of manufactures, and to hasten their departure.
The most specious argument produced against granting a
free trade to the sister kingdom was, that, having labour
cheap, and not being burthened with a poor's rate, she
would be able to undersell us in the market, and thereby
ruin our manufactures. Should England repeal the present laws, and make a better provision for the frugal, the
sober, and the industrious, among the poor, Ireland could
no longer boast of this advantage.

Manufactures always seek the cheapest countries. As
they are leaving the southern countries and travelling to
the north, so in time will they leave the north, and, to a
considerable degree, quit the kingdom, unless some wise
regulations are established for the better relief and government of the labouring poor.

The poor laws to a certain degree discourage improvements in agriculture; for it is certain, that more waste
land would be taken into tillage, if gentlemen were not
alarmed by the increasing burthen of the poor. Against
the claims of the church, provision has been made by an
exemption from tythes for seven years; but the demands
of the poor admit of no exemption. Monied men have
greatly the advantage over the owners and occupiers of
land, as being free from those heavy taxes, which the latter
pay to the king, to the church, and to the poor. When the
poor's rate amounts to ten shillings, or even to four shillings in the pound, who will be at the expence of clearing,
fencing, breaking up, manuring, cropping, the waste and
barren parts of an estate? Certainly no gentlemen can do
it with a view to profit. In Scotland the sums are immense
which have been expended for this purpose; but in England a man of property would choose rather to take the
public for his debtor, than to be himself a debtor to the
poor; more especially as it is not possible for him to con-
jecture what will be the extent of this unlimited rent-
charge upon his estate. Were it not for this incumbrance

agriculture would certainly be pushed much farther than it has ever been, and many thousand acres of the poorer commons, heaths, and moors, would be inclosed and cultivated. The best writers have complained, that by a tax, similar in its operation to our poor's tax, agriculture in France has been depressed, the assessment being made in proportion to their stock in trade. The conduct of the French in this respect is not more absurd than ours. How widely different has been the operation of our land-tax! It has been a spur to industry, because from the beginning the proportion has been never changed. To be consistent in principle, the legislature should either limit the sum to be collected for the poor, or if agriculture is to be effectually checked, they should equalize the land-tax. Had this tax followed our improvements with a tight grasp, and with a watchful eye, like the church, and like the poor, England would not at this day discover the smiling aspect which all foreigners admire, when they every where behold our vallies cloathed with flocks, and our hills with corn. A wise politician will study to remove every obstacle which can retard the progress of improvement: but such is the system of our laws, that the greater the distress among the poor, the less will be the inducement to cultivate our more stubborn and unprofitable lands.

SECT. VI

A DISTINGUISHED writer of the present century has clearly stated some advantages which the community derives from the introduction of luxury, and would from thence conclude, that private vices are public benefits.

His conclusion we cannot grant him; nor can we allow the premises, if by luxury be meant any thing inconsistent with morality. If in our idea of luxury we include only the comforts and conveniences of life, then a taste for luxury must be productive of industry and virtue, must increase the happiness of individuals, and promote the welfare of the state. If men were contented to go naked, to lie under hedges, and, according to the fiction of the poets, to feed on acorns, there would be none to labour till the acorns were consumed. In general the industry of man bears proportion to his real or imaginary wants. Could the landlord be contented with the produce of his native soil, he would cultivate only what would be sufficient for the consumption of his family; or could the labourer be contented with what was barely sufficient to satisfy his hunger, when he no longer felt the cravings of his appetite, he would cease to labour. But as their wants are multiplied, the master is willing to employ more workmen, and the workman himself is reconciled to constant labour. There was a time when the inhabitants of Europe had neither rum, brandy, spices, tea, sugar, nor tobacco: they now covet these, and these new desires have produced new efforts to gratify them. There was a time when they had neither linen, shoes, nor stockings; they now feel the want of these, and receive them as the rewards of industry. But supposing that, with these new desires, they could obtain not only linen, shoes, and stockings, but spices, spirits, tea, sugar, and tobacco, without care or labour, what encouragement would they have to industry? By the present system of our poor laws, at least as they are now administered, the benefits which arise from luxury, in promoting industry among the labouring poor, are lost; and the most improvident may rest assured, that he shall, at all events, share these superfluities with the most active and laborious; and that in times of scarcity his wants shall be the *first* supplied, and his comfort the *first* consulted. To be consistent, the legislature should make the same provision for farmers, manufacturers, and merchants; that in case, by their profusion or neglect of business, they should be insolvent, their debts might all be paid, and themselves, together with their families, might be supported in the stile and manner to which they had been accustomed; all out of the revenues of the state, or by special rates to be collected; not by voluntary donations, but by compulsive payments, and not merely from the opulent, but from those who had themselves been struggling with poverty and want: nay, to be consistent, they should pass a law that no man should reap the fruit of his indiscretion; or, to be perfectly consistent, they should repeal all penal statutes.

Hesiod, in his Georgics, or didactic poem on agriculture, describes with beautiful simplicity the excellent effects of emulation, representing two kinds of strife and contention among men; the one productive of violence, the other of peace, harmony, and plenty. The one is intent only upon plunder, whilst the other seeing wealth as attendant upon industry, is induced to labour, in order to obtain those comforts which the diligent only can command.

Εις ετερον γαρ τις τε ιδων εργοιο χατιζων
Πλουσιον, ος σπευδει μεν αρομμεναι ηδε φυτευειν,
Οικον τ'ευ θεσθαι· ζηλοι δε τε γειτονα γειτων
Εις αφενον σπευδοντ'· αγαθη δ'ερις ηδε βροτοισι.
                                        Ε και Ημ. 21.

This principle has been perverted by our laws; and now the person who excites the envy and emulation of the lazy and improvident, is not the man who by his activity is acquiring affluence, but the indolent poor in every parish, who by his impudence and by his importunity has obtained the most ample and the most unmerited relief. This our poet has described as the natural emulation among beggars. Και πτωχος πτωχω φθονεει.

SECT. VII

IT seems to be a law of nature, that the poor should be to a certain degree improvident, that there may always be some to fulfil the most servile, the most sordid, and the most ignoble offices in the community. The stock of human happiness is thereby much increased, whilst the more delicate are not only relieved from drudgery, and freed from those occasional employments which would make them miserable, but are left at liberty, without interruption, to pursue those callings which are suited to their various dispositions, and most useful to the state. As for the lowest of the poor, by custom they are reconciled to the meanest occupations, to the most laborious works, and to the most hazardous pursuits; whilst the hope of their reward makes them chearful in the midst of all their dangers and their toils. The fleets and armies of a state would soon be in want of soldiers and of sailors, if sobriety and diligence universally prevailed: for what is it but distress and poverty which can prevail upon the lower classes of the people to encounter all the horrors which await them on the tempestuous ocean, or in the field of battle? Men who are easy in their circumstances are not among the foremost to engage in a seafaring or military life. There must be a degree of pressure, and that which is attended with the least violence will be the best. When hunger is either felt or feared, the desire of obtaining bread will quietly dispose the mind to undergo the greatest hardships, and will sweeten the severest labours. The peasant with a sickle in his hand is happier than the prince upon his throne.

Now a fixed, a certain, and a constant provision for the poor weakens this spring; it increases their improvidence, but does not promote their chearful compliance with those demands, which the community is obliged to make on the most indigent of its members; it tends to destroy the harmony and beauty, the symmetry and order of that system, which God and nature have established in the world. The improvident among the poor have been advancing in their claims: they now begin to understand that they have a legal right to all. When this, which hitherto has been only felt, shall be clearly seen, and universally acknowledged, nothing will remain but to cast lots, who among the active and the virtuous shall perform the vilest offices for the indolent and vicious.

SECT. VIII

OUR poor laws are not only unjust, oppressive, and impolitic, nor are they merely by accident inadequate to the purpose for which they were designed; but they proceed upon principles which border on absurdity, as professing to accomplish that which, in the very nature and constitution of the world, is impracticable. They say, that in England no man, even though by his indolence, improvidence, prodigality, and vice, he may have brought himself to poverty, shall ever suffer want. In the progress of society, it will be found, that some must want; and then the only question will be this, Who is most worthy to suffer cold and hunger, the prodigal or the provident, the slothful or the diligent, the virtuous or the vicious? In the South Seas there is an island, which from the first discoverer is called Juan Fernandez. In this sequestered spot, John Fernando placed a colony of goats, consisting of one male, attended by his female. This happy couple finding pasture in abundance, could readily obey the first commandment, to increase and multiply, till in process of time they had replenished their little island*. In advancing to this period they were strangers to misery and want, and seemed to glory in their numbers: but from this unhappy moment they began to suffer hunger; yet continuing for a time to increase their numbers, had they been endued with reason, they must have apprehended the extremity of famine. In this situation the weakest first gave way, and plenty was again restored. Thus they fluctuated between happiness and misery, and either suffered want or rejoiced in abundance, according as their numbers were diminished or increased; never at a stay, yet nearly balancing at all times their quantity of food. This degree of aequipoise was from time to time destroyed, either by epidemical diseases or by the arrival of some vessel in distress. On such occasions their numbers were considerably reduced; but to compensate for this alarm, and to comfort them for the loss of their companions, the survivors never failed immediately to meet returning plenty. They were no longer in fear of famine: they ceased to regard each other with an evil eye; all had abundance, all were contented, all were happy. Thus, what might have been considered as misfortunes, proved a source of comfort; and, to them at least, partial evil was universal good.

When the Spaniards found that the English privateers resorted to this island for provisions, they resolved on the total extirpation of the goats, and for this purpose they put on shore a greyhound dog and bitch†. These in their turn increased and multiplied, in proportion to the quan-

* Dampier, Vol. i. Part ii. p. 88.
† Ulloa, B. ii. C. 4.

tity of food they met with; but in consequence, as the Spaniards had foreseen, the breed of goats diminished. Had they been totally destroyed, the dogs likewise must have perished. But as many of the goats retired to the craggy rocks, where the dogs could never follow them, descending only for short intervals to feed with fear and circumspection in the vallies, few of these, besides the careless and the rash, became a prey; and none but the most watchful, strong, and active of the dogs could get a sufficiency of food. Thus a new kind of balance was established. The weakest of both species were among the first to pay the debt of nature; the most active and vigorous preserved their lives. It is the quantity of food which regulates the numbers of the human species. In the woods, and in the *savage state*, there can be few inhabitants; but of these there will be only a proportionable few to suffer want. As long as food is plenty they will continue to increase and multiply; and every man will have ability to support his family, or to relieve his friends, in proportion to his activity and strength. The weak must depend upon the precarious bounty of the strong; and, sooner or later, the lazy will be left to suffer the natural consequence of their indolence. Should they introduce a community of goods, and at the same time leave every man at liberty to marry, they would at first increase their numbers, but not the sum total of their happiness, till by degrees, all being equally reduced to want and misery, the weakly would be the first to perish.

To procure a more ample, certain, and regular supply of food, should they cut down their woods and take to *breeding cattle*, this plenty would be of long continuance; but in process of time its limits would be found. The most active would acquire property, would have numerous flocks and numerous families; whilst the indolent would either starve or become servants to the rich, and the community would continue to enlarge till it had found its natural bounds, and balanced the quantity of food.

Should they proceed to *agriculture*, these bounds would be much extended, and require ages before the straitness would be felt again. In process of time a compleat division of labour would take place, and they would have not only husbandmen, but artists, manufacturers, and merchants, monied men and gentlemen of landed property, soldiers and men of letters, with all their servants, to exchange their various commodities and labours for the produce of the soil. A noble author, in the north of Britain, is of opinion, that "a nation can scarce be too populous for husbandry, as agriculture has the singular property of producing food in proportion to the number of consumers*." But is it not clear, that when all that is fertile has been cultivated to the highest pitch of industry, the progress must of necessity be stopped, and that when the human species shall have multiplied in proportion to this increase of food, it can proceed no further? Indeed, as we have remarked already of the savage state, should they establish a community of goods, their numbers for a time would certainly increase; but the quantity of food not being augmented in proportion, and that which had been sufficient only for a given number being now distributed to the increasing multitude, all would have too little, and the weakly would perish sooner than if he who tilled the soil had been left to reap the undivided fruits of his industry and labour. Nations may for a time increase their numbers beyond the due proportion of their food, but they will in the same proportion destroy the ease and comfort of the affluent, and, without any possible advantage, give universality to that misery and want, which had been only partial. The course of nature may be easily disturbed, but man will never be able to reverse its laws.

* Sketches on Man, P. 56.

The earth is no where more fertile than it is in China, nor does any country abound so much in people; yet the cries of deserted children prove, that even they have found limits to their population. Few countries have been more productive than the land of Canaan was; a land described as flowing with milk and honey, fertile in corn, and rich in pastures: yet even in the land of Canaan they had many poor; and it was said to them, but not in the way of threatening, "the poor shall never cease from among you*." Indeed it was impossible they ever should, because whilst men have appetites and passions, what but distress and poverty can stop the progress of population? The inhabitants of Europe are said to have doubled their numbers every five hundred years: from which we may infer that their quantity of food has been doubled in these periods. Throughout America, for the same reason, they have been doubled every five-and-twenty years; and in some colonies, in the space of fifteen years.

If a new and equal division of property were made in England, we cannot doubt that the same inequality which we now observe would soon take place again: the improvident, the lazy, and the vicious, would dissipate their substance; the prudent, the active, and the virtuous, would again increase their wealth. If the legislature were to make this distribution, the evil would not be equal to the injustice of the measure: things would soon return into their proper channel, order and subordination would be again restored, diligence would be encouraged, and the virtuous would be fed. But by establishing a permanent community of goods, and neither increasing the quantity of food, nor limiting the number of those who are to share it, they divert the occasional surplus of national wealth from the industrious to the lazy, they increase the number of unprofitable citizens, and sow the seeds of

* Deut. xv. 11.

misery for the whole community; increasing the general
distress, and causing more to die for want, than if poverty
had been left to find its proper channel.

It is well known that our commons, without stint,
starve all our cattle. Here we clearly see the natural effects
of that community of goods, which the poor laws would
render universal. In the infancy of the Christian church,
this experiment was fairly tried; but even whilst the
Apostles, blest with a perfect knowledge of the human
heart, were yet alive, it was found to be intolerable. We
have adopted it in England; and what has been the consequence? Are poverty and wretchedness unknown? or
rather, are not poverty and wretchedness increasing daily,
in exact proportion with our efforts to restrain them? One
of the neatest writers of the English nation, who under-
stood this subject, has well observed, "the sufferings of
the poor are less known than their misdeeds: they starve,
and freeze, and rot among themselves; but they beg, and
steal, and rob among their betters. There is not a parish in
the liberty of Westminster, which doth not raise thou-
sands annually for the poor; and there is not a street in
that liberty, which doth not swarm all day with beggars,
and all night with thieves." His expression is nervous, his
description animated; but even the simple truth, when
divested of all its ornaments, must excite astonishment.
The effect is striking; but the cause of this phaenomenon
will be evident to those only who can examine it with a
fixed attention.

There is a parish in the West of England which has
never wanted poor, and in which, excepting for one short
period, the poor have never wanted work; yet their poverty
and misery have uniformly advanced constantly, out-
stripping all efforts which have been made to provide for
their distress. The farmers at this time pay ten shillings
in the pound on the improved rents; yet wretchedness

seems to have taken up its residence in every cottage, and the most miserable are they whose gains have been the greatest.

SECT. IX

ON the subject of population we have had warm disputes, whilst some have lamented that our numbers are decreasing, and others with confidence have boasted that our population has rapidly advanced; all seeming to be agreed, that the wealth of a country consists in the number of its inhabitants. When industry and frugality keep pace with population, or rather when population is only the consequence of these, the strength and riches of a nation will bear proportion to the number of its citizens: but when the increase of people is unnatural and forced, when it arises only from a community of goods, it tends to poverty and weakness. In respect to population, some countries will reach their ne plus ultra sooner, and some later, according as they surmount the obstacles which impede their progress. This period can be retarded by improvements in agriculture, by living harder or by working more, by extensive conquests or by increasing commerce.

The cultivation of rice in China enabled them to feed some millions of people, more than could have been maintained by any other grain; whereas in the highlands of Scotland, where neither rice nor yet wheat will grow, the inhabitants soon became a burthen to the soil. Their chief dependance for supporting the present population is on frugality, and constant, steady, unremitted labour, without any hope of being able to advance their numbers. Oatmeal and water, with a little milk, is their common food, and to procure this they work as long as they can see. They till the soil; they watch their cattle; and, at their leisure hours, they spin all the linen and the woollen which their families consume.

The Romans, even when they had lost their domestic industry and habits of economy, were able to feed their increasing citizens by tribute from the distant provinces, as the Spaniards do by purchasing provisions with the gold and silver of Peru. The Dutch have no other refuge but in good government, industry, and commerce, for which their situation is most favourable. Their pastures are rich, but not sufficient to maintain half the number of their inhabitants, who are employed and fed by every nation upon earth, but reside in Holland for the convenience of the water-carriage, the security of their persons, and the protection of their property.

When a country is so far advanced in population as to be distressed for food; and when the forementioned resources have been exhausted, it has then reached its utmost limits; and in such a case, against increasing want there can be two remedies only which are natural, and one unnatural: for either none must marry, but they who can maintain a family, or else all who are in distress must emigrate. If these natural remedies are rejected, it can remain only for the poor to expose their children the moment they are born, which is the horrid practice adopted in the richest country upon earth to preserve the community from famine. With regard to celibacy, we may observe, that where things are left to a course of nature, one passion regulates another, and the stronger appetite restrains the weaker. There is an appetite, which is and should be urgent, but which, if left to operate without restraint, would multiply the human species before provision could be made for their support. Some check, some balance is therefore absolutely needful, and hunger is the proper balance; hunger, not as directly felt, or feared by the individual for himself, but as foreseen and feared for his immediate offspring. Were it not for this the equilibrium would not be preserved so near as it is at present in the world, between the numbers of people and the quantity of food. Various are the circumstances to be observed in different nations, which tend to blunt the shafts of Cupid, or at least to quench the torch of Hymen. In many parts of Europe we see multitudes of both sexes, not from policy, but from superstition and religious prejudice, bound by irrevocable vows of chastity. In other parts we hear of numbers who are compelled to spend their days in a seraglio, where it is not to be expected that all should be prolific; whilst in consequence of this unjustifiable practice, a corresponding number must pass through the world without leaving a representative behind them. But in every country, at least on this side the Atlantic Ocean, we find a similar effect from prudence; and without the assistance of either a seraglio, or a convent, the younger branches of the best families have been left to wither. In every country multitudes would marry, if they had a comfortable prospect for themselves, and for their children; but if all should listen to this call of nature, deaf to a louder call, the whole world in a few years would be distressed with famine. Yet, even in such a case, when it is impolitic that all should marry, this should be wholly left to every man's discretion, and to that balance of the appetites which nature has established. But if, notwithstanding the restraints of distress and poverty, they who are not able to maintain a family will yet marry, there can be no resource but in emigration. In the highlands of Scotland, when the inhabitants became a burthen to the soil, they tried every possible expedient; and, when all others failed, their young men with reluctance turned their back upon a country which was not able to support them. It is well known that their emigrations are considerable. They do not issue forth in assembled multitudes, like swarms from the northern hives of old; nor do they, like a torrent, overflow and desolate the adjacent countries; but, like the silent dew, they drop upon the richest pastures, and wandering to the remotest corners of the earth in quest of food, with the industry of bees they collect their honey from the most luxuriant flowers. These active, hardy, and laborious people, are to be found in the temperate, in the torrid, and in the frigid zones, in every island, and on every habitable mountain of Europe, Asia, Africa, and America. Yet in their native country the numbers never fail: the supply is constant. Now, if, instead of collecting for themselves wherever food is to be found, these wanderers had been equally supported on their barren mountains by contributions from the more fertile vallies of the South, can we imagine that the births in Scotland would be fewer than they are at present? The overflowings of their population might have been accelerated, but could not thereby have been retarded. Having no contributions from the South, they have quitted their country, and made room for others. We are told, upon the best authority*, that in the highlands of Scotland, a woman will bring twenty children into the world, and rear only two. Had she sufficient food for more, more would live. The women there, like the women in all countries which are come to their utmost height of population, are more prolific than the soil. To provide more food on their bleak and barren mountains, is beyond a question. But if now, to rear these twenty children, a poor's rate were to be collected in more fertile countries, yet in countries which are fully peopled in proportion to their labour and to the produce of the soil, is it not evident, that the scarcity and distress would only be transferred, and that the children of the South must die, that the children of the North might live? But supposing these should live; yet at best they could only take the place of those that died, and

* Smith, Wealth of Nations.

more women in the North would increase and multiply, till they felt the same degree of pressure which they feel at present. Neither Switzerland nor the coast of Africa are depopulated by emigrations, because the quantity of food in each remains unaltered. It is with the human species as with all other articles of trade without a premium; the demand will regulate the market.

By establishing a community of goods, or rather by giving to the idle and to the vicious the *first* claim upon the produce of the earth, many of the more prudent, careful, and industrious citizens are straitened in their circumstances, and restrained from marriage. The farmer breeds only from the best of all his cattle; but our laws choose rather to preserve the worst, and seem to be anxious lest the breed should fail. The cry is, Population, population! population at all events! But is there any reasonable fear of depopulation? We have seen that corn upon an average has been considerably cheaper since the commencement of the present century, than it was for an equal term before; yet wages have been raised in the proportion of six to four, and the rent of land is doubled. May we not infer from hence, that the produce of the soil must have increased nearly in the same proportions. If we consider the improvements which have been made in agriculture, by clearing woods, inclosing wastes, draining morasses, laying the common fields in severalty, and making roads; by the introduction of clover, saintfoin, turneps, and potatoes; by the breaking up of extensive downs; and by the superior skill of the present race in the management of all sorts of land, with respect to stocking, manuring, cropping, not forgetting their superior weight of capital to work with; we shall cease to wonder at this vast increase of produce. But is it possible that the produce should be thus increased, and not the people also who consume it? We need not desire any man to visit London, Norwich, Bath, Bristol, Hull, Liverpool, Leeds, Wakefield, Manchester, and Birmingham; we need not call upon him to view our mines of coal, copper, lead, iron, and tin, with all the new manufactures which depend on these: but let him at least count our flocks, and calculate the quantity of corn produced by recent improvements in our tillage; then let him ask himself if our population is increased.

Whilst food is to be had, there is no fear of wanting people. But should the population of a country get beyond the produce of the soil, and of the capital engaged in trade, how shall these people find employment? Whenever this shall be the case, the evil will increase, and the capital will go on constantly diminishing; like as in private life, when a gentleman breaks in upon his principal to pay the ordinary expences of his family. When a trading nation is obliged to spend more than the revenue which is derived from commerce, and not from accident, but as the effect of some abiding cause, exceeds continually the profit of its trade, without some substantial reformation, the ruin of that nation will be inevitable. Should the capital itself accumulate, the interest of money would be lowered, the demand for labour would increase, and the superlucration on this increase of trade would continue to enlarge the capital. Speculation apart, it is a fact, that in England we have more than we can feed, and many more than we can profitably employ under the present system of our laws.

SECT. X

ALL the effects which I have been describing, have not been fully felt. Let it however be remembered, that a distinction must be made between those evils which have already been severely felt, and the greater evils which in

the course of nature and due time may be expected. The
tendency of a law may be most destructive; yet, by ad-
ventitious circumstances, the bad consequences may be
checked and prevented for a season. It is not to be imag-
ined that men, who by close application and watchful attention to their business, by rigid frugality and hard
labour, have made a decent provision for their families,
should freely part with a considerable proportion of their
property, or suffer it to be taken from them without
strong efforts to retain it. For more than a century the
struggles have been obstinate and unremitted, yet for
more than a century the poor's rates have been constantly
increasing. From time to time, as men remarked the rapidity of this progress, their exertions were more than
common, and some transient reformation was effected.
When at last they found, that they had no other way
remaining to protect the fruits of industry from the ex-
travagant demands of indolence, and from the undis-
tinguishing benevolence of power, they adopted, from
necessity and not from choice, the miserable expedient of
building workhouses. Till these are completely filled, and
even after they are full, they serve a double purpose: they
disarm the magistrate, they intimidate the poor.

As the law now stands, the parish officers, in certain
cases, may build houses on the waste for the reception of
the impotent and aged; but they have been hitherto so
prudent as not to exercise a power, which would be destructive to themselves, without being beneficial to the
poor. Happily the justices of peace have no legal authority
to augment the number of our cottages. There can be no
compulsion in this case. Some of them indeed have indirectly attempted this, but they have been resisted by the
more provident and wary in most parishes. Hence the
number of houses becomes a gage, at once to measure and
to regulate the extent of population. In every village will
be found plenty of young men and women, who only wait

for habitations to lay the foundation of new families, and who with joy would hasten to the altar, if they could be certain of a roof to shelter them at night. It has been chiefly from the want of houses that the poor have not more rapidly increased. If the most opulent parishes in the kingdom were obliged to find habitations, as they are to provide work, or food and raiment for the poor, they would be themselves reduced in a course of years to such extreme distress, that all moveable stock would be carried off, the land would be left uncultivated, the houses would go to ruin, and the poor would starve. As the rents have been advancing, new houses have been built; but hitherto the progress has been retarded by the superior values of money in the public funds. Should the present law subsist, the value of land will sink, and the rent of cottages will rise; each in proportion to the burthen of the poor, and the demand for houses. It is true, by a statute made in the thirty-first year of Queen Elizabeth, there is a penalty on every person who shall build a cottage without assigning four acres of land to be held for ever with it; but this statute, with which her famous poor law is in perfect harmony, and which, if observed, would have prevented the greatest evils felt and to be feared from the unlimited provision for the poor, has been long neglected, or perhaps was never regarded. The penalty is ten pounds for the first erection of the cottage, and forty shillings per month as long as it shall be occupied. Had this law remained in force, or had it been constantly observed, the poor would not have multiplied; but then the manufactures would not have flourished in the kingdom as they do at present. Under this law it is evident, that no poor man could marry till there was a cottage vacant to receive him; for no inmates were allowed.

The last circumstance which remains to be assigned, as having checked and prevented for a season the evil consequences resulting from our poor laws, is the shame and reproach of being relieved by a parish: but these have long since ceased to operate. It is high time, therefore, that more effectual provision should be made for the protection of industry in affluence, and for the relief of industry in the seasons of distress.

SECT. XI

THE best politicians in Europe have condemned the present system of our poor laws. Among these we may reckon two great and distinguished writers; one universally admired for his incomparable work on the spirit of laws; the other for his most elegant and judicious comment on the laws of England. A nobleman, who stands foremost among the literati in the north of Britain, has more freely and more fully delivered his opinion, and perfectly coincides in sentiment with those able lawyers. These respectable authors have condemned the principles, whilst others have blamed only the execution of our laws. But all who are even in the least degree acquainted with the subject have lamented, that two millions should be annually expended on the poor without relieving their distress.

SECT. XII

IF it were possible to meet with proper persons to execute our laws, they would not be so hurtful to the community as they are at present. But where shall we find men qualified to be at once trustees and guardians for the public and for the poor? An overseer should be endued with more than common patience; willing to hear with calmness and composure the complaints of the most untoward and perverse; blest with a command of temper such as few possess. He should be diligent and active, that he may visit the habitations of the poor, and examine with his own eyes the nature, the extent, and the cause of their distress. He should be a man of good understanding, sharp, sensible, and well-informed, that he may know what is the best, the cheapest, and the most effectual method, at once to relieve and to employ the poor. He should be a man of penetration, quick in discerning, and ready in detecting the false pretences of impostors. He should be a man of the most humane and compassionate disposition; not merely that he may shed the sympathizing tear, but that he may exert himself to the utmost to comfort and support the sick, and properly to sweeten the bitter cup for those who are drinking the dregs of life. He should be at the same time a man of firmness and resolution; not to be worn out and teazed into compliance, nor yet to be moved either by threats or by deceitful tears. He should be inexorably just, considering the public fund, out of which he is to relieve the poor, as a most sacred deposit committed to his care, in confidence that he will administer it to the best of his judgment and ability. He should be a man of a disinterested and honest disposition, that, in the discharge of this important trust, he may neither directly nor indirectly defraud the public, either to favour his friends or to promote his trade. In one word, if in him should centre all the excellencies, which are scattered with a sparing hand among the human race; if he had no other trade, occupation, or pursuit which required his attention; if, thus qualified, he were willing to give up his time for the benefit of the public, and for the comfort of the poor; if a succession of such were to be found, and if their power were supreme, subject to no controul from the interference of a magistrate; the burthen might yet be tolerable, and some of the evils, naturally attendant on the present system of our poor laws, instead of being severely felt, would for the present be seen only at a distance.

Many parishes have been sensible of this difficulty, more especially in the cloathing counties: but as if, whilst they severely felt it, they had only indistinctly seen it, they have made application to parliament, complaining that the business was too much for the attendance and attention of four overseers; and therefore praying, that one additional overseer might be appointed with absolute and sole authority to grant relief. Their argument appears to be absurd, but their meaning is precise and clear. They would be thus at liberty to choose the most proper person for the charge; and he, having little else to do, could pay more attention to the business. The event has in some measure answered their expectation; but, at best, this can be considered only as a good expedient to palliate one of those many bad effects which flow from a pernicious law.

SECT. XIII

TO remedy these evils, various have been the schemes recommended to the public, by men who have been revered for the strength of their understandings, the extent of their knowledge, and the uprightness of their intentions. They have chiefly recommended palliatives; and such only have been tried, yet with little or with no effect. They have indeed checked the evil for a time, and only for a time, to return with accumulated force: for, notwithstanding all their efforts, the tax collected to relieve the poor is swelled in many places from ten or twelve pounds annually to five hundred pounds a year, where no manufactures have been established; and in the manufacturing parishes, from little or nothing to fifteen hundred, two thousand, and even three thousand pounds a year.

The legislature began with requiring the consent of two justices of peace, before the overseers could have power to relieve the poor*. They then insisted that none should be relieved, but those who were put upon the list by the parishioners assembled in their vestry, or by authority under the hand of a justice†. After this it was enacted, that no justice of peace should grant an order, without having examined upon oath the party making application to him for relief‡. Upon all these conditions we hear the legislature constantly complaining that the evil still went on increasing.

The expedient which has been most often tried, has been to compel both the pauper and his family to wear the Roman P in scarlet cloth upon their shoulders§; and from this much was expected, but in vain. It has operated, indeed, as a partial repeal of a bad law, repealing however all that could be considered as valuable, and leaving all that is noxious to the state; discouraging only the ingenuous, the modest, and the meek, that there may be the more for those who, lost to shame, have long since forgot to blush. Of all human inventions, none can be more cruel than this. You invite the poor, you offer him relief, but you will give it only upon this condition, that he shall receive it with a mark of infamy. The overseers are liable to a fine, if they do not impose this mark upon the indigent; but such is their humanity, that they risk the penalty rather than reproach the wretched with his poverty. Should they give this badge to some, they must impose it upon all. The worthless and the impudent

* 43 Eliz.
† 3 and 4 W. and M.
‡ 9 Geo. I, c. 7.
§ 8 and 9 W. c. 30. f. 2.

would not regard it; the modest would sooner die than wear it. There is no doubt that time would reconcile them to it, more especially when they saw none or few without it; but then, what purpose would it answer? Whilst it took effect, it would be hurtful: when it ceased to operate, it would be useless.

Finding the futility of this device, the most common refuge has been to parochial and provincial workhouses; against which there appear insuperable objections. It was thought, that with watchful attention the poor would do more work under one roof, and be fed much cheaper, than when dispersed in their several cottages. An expectation, however, which experience has never yet confirmed. Even in parochial workhouses, and in those which are under the best regulation, the poor do so little work, that the produce of their labour almost escapes our notice, whilst they are maintained at a most enormous expence. In their cottages they might live comfortably on the average of four pounds each; whereas under the management of the public they cost from five to ten, and even twelve pounds each, per annum. It is not reasonable to imagine, that men, deprived of liberty, will work for others with the same chearful activity as when working for themselves; or that they will be contented with the hard and homely fare, which they could eat with thankfulness, whilst as freemen they were surrounded with their friends. It is hope that must sweeten all our labours. Let a man have no pursuit, no exercise for his hopes and fears, and you may as well take the marrow from his bones, which was designed by nature to supple all his joints. You may feed him well; but, without making him a more useful member in society, you will leave him to drag on a miserable existence, a burthen to himself and to the public. It is now a maxim universally received, that the service of a slave is the dearest service which can be had. Let a man consult his own feelings, and the reason will be obvious.

The terror of being sent to a workhouse acts like an abolition of the poor's tax on all who dread the loss of liberty. It is in effect a virtual repeal, as far as it extends, of those laws, which should long since have given place to better regulations. But unfortunately the most worthy objects suffer most by this repeal, and the advantage to the public is little more than negative. The quiet and the cleanly dread the noise and nastiness, even more than the confinement of a workhouse. They pant for the pure and wholesome air, which they can never hope to breathe where numbers are confined within narrow limits, and sigh for that serenity and peace, which they must despair to find where the most profligate of the human species are met together. By the fear of being sentenced to such society, many, who deserve a better fate, struggle with poverty till they sink under the burthen of their misery. Against county workhouses, improperly called houses of industry, the objections are much stronger. The buildings, the furniture, the salaries, the waste, and the imposition, every thing is upon a large and expensive scale, without its being possible to preserve, for any length of time, a system of economy. At first, indeed, there might be great exertion; but the novelty being over, few gentlemen would be found public spirited enough to continue their attendance and attention to a business in which, as individuals, they would be so little interested, and for which they must give up more important or more pleasant engagements and pursuits. By experience it is found, that without reckoning interest upon the prime cost of either furniture or buildings, the poor in these extensive establishments are not maintained for less than I have stated. But whilst the experience is so enormous, are they happy? Far from happy, they are wretched. With all the discomforts of a parochial workhouse, they feel themselves in a hopeless state of banishment from their relations and connections. It is true, they eat, they drink, and they are miserable. This kind of banishment has the same effect in part as a repeal of the poor laws, because few are willing to be thus relieved. These houses of industry cannot be vindicated, either in point of comfort or economy: if they have therefore any merit, it can be only that kind of merit which I have stated; and if it be wise to have recourse to them, it would be much wiser directly to repeal the laws, against the depredations of which these houses are to protect your property. A county workhouse, at best, may be considered as a colony to which a few of the superabundant members of the community have been transported to make room for others; or it may be considered as a new manufacture, beneficial in its progress to employ the idle hands; beneficial, if it were possible to make a profit on their labour; yet like other manufactures, under the present system of our laws, increasing the number and the distresses of the poor.

That gentlemen of landed property should have taken the alarm, and that all who feel the burthen of the poor should wish to be relieved, is not to be wondered at. Yet surely we may be permitted to express astonishment, that when in the year 1775 the House of Commons were to provide a remedy for the growing evil, no expedient should present itself, but to erect county workhouses.

> They resolved, 1. That the laws relating to the poor are defective, and the good purposes intended by them in many respects prevented.
>
> 2. That the money raised for the relief of the poor is a grievous, and, if no new regulations are made, will be an increasing burthen upon the public.

They then recommended county workhouses, leaving the parishes at liberty to draw at discretion on the county stock, for the relief of such as were not proper objects for a workhouse.

The counties, however, were not weak enough to accept an offer which must have entailed a tax of four shillings in the pound on their estates for ever, without procuring any benefit to the public, to the land-owner, to the farmer, or to the poor.

Another experient, and the last which I shall mention, is the most abominable that ever was invented: it is to farm the poor. In some parishes they are farmed at so much an head, but in others the contract is for a given sum. In one parish in Gloucestershire a contractor had agreed to take all the expence of the poor upon himself for a very moderate consideration. Taking the present numbers in confinement, he has only two shillings a week for each; yet out of this he is to be at the charge of all litigations and removals, and to relieve all others who are not proper objects for a workhouse, and after all to make a profit for himself.

All these expedients have the same tendency. They are adopted with a professed intention to lower the poor rates; and it is confessed, that many are thereby deterred from making application for relief, who would otherwise be a burthen to the public. But then is not this a partial, impolitic, oppressive repeal of a bad law, without reducing the tax; for it continues to increase, and without making a better provision for those among the poor who are most worthy of attention?

Having thus endeavoured to display the imperfections which are most obvious in our management of the poor, let us now examine the provision made for their relief by other nations.

In the early ages of the world there could be no great difficulty in this matter, as the quantity of food was more than could be consumed. In process of time, when property had got footing in the world, they, who had neither flocks nor herds, became slaves, and, selling themselves for bread, together with their children, constituted the principal treasure of the rich. When the rich had so far increased their stock, that their cattle had not sufficient room to feed, they quitted their ancient habitations, and sought new settlements. Thus it is said, that Abraham was very rich in cattle, that he had sheep and oxen, and men servants and maid servants, and camels and asses, and silver and gold. The same nearly was the prosperity of Lot. But when the land was not able to bear them with their flocks and with their herds, they agreed to part, and Lot chose for himself the plains of Jordan. When the offspring of Abraham settled in the land of Canaan, they continued the same mode of relieving the distressed, only with this exception, that in the seventh year the poor, who had sold himself, was to go out free. This custom of exchanging their liberty for bread was followed by most of the nations upon earth, and was the general practice of the world, till Christianity prevailed, and became the established religion of the Roman empire. The milder genius of this religion, which proclaims liberty to the captive, and the opening of the prison doors to them that are bound, abhorrent to slavery in all its forms, has almost banished that cruel custom from our world; and in its stead has made the best possible provision for the poor, leaving them to be supported by the free bounty of the rich. It is true, the mistaken zeal of its first converts, inflamed by the expectation of that transcendent glory which the gospel had revealed to them, poured contempt upon their visible possessions of houses and of lands. These they sold, and being all of one heart, and of one soul, they agreed to have all things common*. But no such community of goods received the sanction of divine authority. When Peter reproached Ananias, it was for his falsehood only: "Whilst the land remained, was it not thine own; and after it was sold, was it not in thine own power†?"

The positive injunctions of the gospel are clear and distinct, and should never have been forgot. "Every man

* Acts iv. 32.
† Acts v. 4.

according as he purposeth in his heart, so let him give; not grudgingly, or of necessity: for God loveth a chearful giver*." These voluntary contributions were collected on the first day of every week, when they assembled at their public worship. The Christian dispensation gives the highest encouragement to the overflowings of benevolence, but at the same time leaves every man at liberty to give or not to give, proceeding upon this maxim, that it should be lawful for a man to do what he will with his own. Whilst however the followers of this religion are left to their own judgment and discretion, they are under the strongest obligations to be liberal in their donations, and to relieve the distresses of their fellow creatures to the utmost of their ability. In the description of the great and final judgment of the world, it is said, "When the Son of man shall come in his glory, and all the holy angels with him, then shall he sit upon the throne of his glory. And before him shall be gathered all nations; and he shall separate them one from another, as a shepherd divideth his sheep from the goats: And he shall set the sheep on his right hand, but the goats on the left. Then shall the King say unto them on his right hand, Come, ye blessed of my Father, inherit the kingdom prepared for you from the foundation of the world. For I was an hungered, and ye gave me meat: I was thirsty, and ye gave me drink: I was a stranger, and ye took me in: naked, and ye clothed me: I was sick, and ye visited me: I was in prison, and ye came unto me. For inasmuch as ye did it unto one of the least of these my brethren, ye did it unto me†." From this description we must not too hastily conclude that the charity of Christians is to be indiscriminate and blind. Among the various objects of distress a choice is to be made, selecting first those which are most worthy, and reserving the residue for those who have nothing but their misery

* 2 Cor. ix. 7.
† Matt. xxv.

to excite compassion. Let the virtuous citizen be fed, then let the profligate and the prodigal share all that prudence and frugality shall have left behind them. To reverse this order is neither politic nor just: for surely nothing can be more inconsistent with equity, than to give the bread of industry to indolence and vice. Christian charity was never meant to discourage diligence and application, nor to promote among men a wanton dissipation of their substance. The Apostle of the Gentiles, both by example and by precept, teaches a lesson which too many among the poor have yet to learn. We hear him thus appealing to his converts: "We did not eat any man's bread for nought; but wrought with labour and travel night and day, that we might not be chargeable to any of you: not because we have not power, but to make ourselves an example unto you to follow us. For even when we were with you, this we commanded you, that if any would not work, neither should he eat*."

For many centuries the nations of Europe had no other way of providing for their increasing poor, when occasional benefactions became inadequate to their wants, but by driving them out, like swarms, to seek new settlements. It was not then difficult for warlike tribes, issuing forth in countless numbers, with their flocks and with their herds, to make an impression, when at any time they turned their arms against the peaceable inhabitants of more cultivated countries. But now that all have quitted the shepherd life and taken to agriculture; now that each nation, although more numerous than formerly, is hemmed in by nations equal to itself in numbers, wealth, and military ardour; it is become necessary to provide for their poor at home. This they have attempted by public hospitals and private benefactions. With regard to hospitals, they find that these only remove the evil for a time, and in the issue extend the bounds of extreme poverty and

* 2 Thess. iii. 8–10.

wretchedness. They at first pleased themselves with the idea, that they had put an end to human misery; but they soon found it returning back upon them, and the vacant places, which had been left by those provided for in their public hospitals, filled up again by objects of distress. When at Lions they opened an hospital with forty beds for the reception of the poor, they could fill only half that number, but now eight hundred beds are not sufficient; and when they built the hospital of Saltpetriere, near Paris, it had few inhabitants, but now they lodge twelve thousand; and yet to their astonishment they find, that instead of having banished distress and poverty, they have increased the number of the poor. The effect has filled them with amazement; but they do not seem to have as yet discovered, that they have been attempting to stop a rapid river in its progress, and to push back the waters of the oceans.

In Holland their chief dependance is on voluntary contributions, and a rigid execution of the laws; and in Holland are to be seen more industry and fewer criminals, than are to be found in the best governed countries in Europe of the same extent.

SECT. XIV

I AM now come to the most arduous part of my undertaking. Some remedy must be found for the growing evil, and those which have been hitherto proposed have been found inadequate. In laying down a plan, I shall begin with establishing the general principles on which we must proceed.

It is evident then, that no system can be good which does not, in the first place, encourage industry, economy, and subordination; and, in the second place, regulate population by the demand for labour.

To promote industry and economy, it is necessary that the relief which is given to the poor should be limited and precarious. "Languescet industria, intendetur socordia, si nullus ex se metus aut spes; et securi omnes aliena subsidia expectabunt, sibi ignavi, nobis graves." No man will be an economist of water, if he can go to the well or to the brook as often as he please; nor will he watch with solicitous attention to keep the balance even between his income and expenditure, if he is sure to be relieved in the time of need. The labouring poor at present are greatly defective, both in respect to industry and economy. Considering the numbers to be maintained, they work too little, they spend too much, and what they spend is seldom laid out to the best advantage. When they return from threshing or from plough, they might card, they might spin, or they might knit. We are told, that one thousand pair of Shetland stockings are annually imported into Leith, of which the price is from five to seven pence a pair: yet labour at Learwick, the small capital of Shetland islands, is ten pence a day. These stockings are made at leisure hours. In these islands they have no dependance but upon their industry and frugality. They consume neither tea, nor sugar, nor spices, because they cannot afford to purchase these useless articles; neither do they wear stockings or shoes, till by their diligence they have acquired such affluence as to bear this expence. How different is theirs from the dress and diet of our common people, who have lost all ideas of economy! If by their industry they could procure these articles of luxury, or if their linen, their cotton, and their silk, were spun, and wove, and knit in their own houses, and at leisure hours, their desire to obtain these things would be advantageous to the state: but surely, if in the colder regions of the North these are not essential to their existence, or even to their happiness, they should be considered in the South only as the rewards of industry, and should never, from the common fund, be given promiscuously to all, as they will inevitably be, unless that fund shall have some other limits besides the wants and expectations of the poor. Unless the degree of pressure be increased, the labouring poor will never acquire habits of diligent application, and of severe frugality. To increase this pressure, the poor's tax must be gradually reduced in certain proportions annually, the sum to be raised in each parish being fixed and certain, not boundless, and obliged to answer unlimited demands. This enormous tax might easily in the space of nine years be reduced nine-tenths; and the remainder being reserved as a permanent supply, the poor might safely be left to the free bounty of the rich, without the interposition of any other law. But if the whole system of compulsive charity were abolished, it would be still better for the state. I am not singular in this opinion. Baron Montesquieu has given his opinion, "Que des secours passages vaudroient mieux que des éstabissemens perpetuels*;" and our own countryman, who had been long conversant with this business, has told us, "I am persuaded that to provide for the poor, who are unable to work, might be safely left to voluntary charity, unenforced by any compulsive law†."

To assist the industrious poor, who have neither tools nor materials, but more especially to train up the children of the dissolute in useful labour, there might be in each parish one or more work-shops, where they might be certain of employment, and of daily pay for the work performed. In these shops they should neither be lodged nor fed, being taught to depend each for himself on his own diligence and patient application to his business. The building, the tools, and the materials, would be all that required assistance from the public fund.

* L. xxiii. C. 29.
† Fielding on Robbers.

The grand resource however should be from the labouring poor themselves, previous to their being incumbered with families. They have throughout the kingdom a number of friendly societies established, which have been productive of good effects, and in some places have reduced the rates. But these societies have more than one defect. All their members contribute equally to the public fund, without respect to their ability, to the proportion of their gains, or to the number of their children. By this regulation some pay too little, others pay too much. The sum, which they deposit weekly, is insignificant and trifling when compared with what it ought to be. But the greatest misfortune is, that they are altogether left to their own option to join these societies or not; in consequence of which liberty, many of these associations for mutual assistance are going to decay. If this be indeed a good expedient, it should be pushed as far as it will go: it should be firmly established, made universal, and subjected to wholesome regulations. The unmarried man should pay one quarter of his wages weekly, and the father of four young children not more than one thirtieth of his income, which is nearly the sum which all contribute to their present clubs. To drive them into these societies, no man should be intitled to relief from the parochial fund who did not belong to one of these. Thus would sobriety, industry, and economy, take place of drunkenness, idleness, and prodigality, and due subordination would be again restored.

As long as it should be found expedient to retain a given proportion of the present poor tax, the disposal of this should be wholly at the discretion of the minister, churchwardens, and overseers, or the majority of them, subject only to the orders of a vestry. By this provision the subordination of the poor would be more effectually secured, and the civil magistrate would be at liberty to bend his whole attention to the preservation of the peace, and to the good government of the people.

This plan would be aided and assisted much by laying a sufficient tax upon the alehouses to reduce their number, these being the principal nurseries for drunkenness, idleness, and vice.

Should things be left thus to flow in their proper channels, the consequence would be, that, as far as it is possible according to the present constitution of the world, our population would be no longer unnatural and forced, but would regulate itself by the demand for labour.

There remains one thing more for the legislature to do, which is to increase the quantity of food. This may be done with ease, by laying a tax upon all horses used in husbandry, gradually increasing this tax till the farmers have returned to the use of oxen. This change would enable England not only to maintain her present population, but greatly to increase it. The land which now supports one horse, in proper working order, would bear two oxen for draft and for the shambles, if not also one cow for the pail; or any two of these, with a man, his wife, and his three children. If we consider the number of horses at present used for husbandry in this island, should only half that number give place to oxen, it would not be easy to calculate, or even to conceive, all the benefits and advantages which the public would derive from this vast increase of food. In many parishes where they have no manufactures, but the cultivation of the soil, the horses consume the produce of more land than the inhabitants themselves require. Suppose a parish to consist of four thousand acres of arable and pasture land; let this be cultivated by one hundred and fifty horses, and let it feed one thousand souls: now if, for the present, we allow only two acres of oats and two of hay for each of the horses, the amount will be six hundred productive acres, which will be more than sufficient to feed the given number of inhabitants. But the fact is, that a horse, to be fully fed, requires five ton of hay, and from thirteen to three-and-twenty quarters of oats, per annum, according to his work. Some farmers allow the former, and the latter is given by the great carriers on the public roads, which would bring the computation to about eight acres each for horses used in husbandry; but then few farmers suffer their horses to be highly fed. If we allow three acres of pasture for each ox or cow, and consider, that in calculating the quantity of land sufficient to maintain a team of horses, the needful fallows must be carried to account, we shall not be at a loss for food, when we have substituted two oxen, and one family of five persons, in the place of every horse.

It must be confessed, that the tax on horses would be apparently a tax on husbandry, but in reality it would only be a tax on pride and prejudice. Neither would it be a tax for the purpose of revenue, which would certainly be most impolitic; but it would be a tax for the regulation of trade, beneficial to the public, and highly advantageous to the farmer. In China they use few cattle in the cultivation of the soil, and therefore they are able to support a more abundant population. By reverting to the antient practice of ploughing with oxen instead of horses, we should enjoy the same advantage; and till the population of our country had found its utmost limits, we should rejoice in affluence.

With the same intentions, the legislature should facilitate the laying common fields in severalty, leaving the inclosure of these lands to every man's discretion. Wherever these allotments have been carried into execution, the value of land has been nearly doubled. Yet, independent of the exertion, the time, and the fatigue, requisite to procure a private act of parliament for this purpose, the expence of the act itself, and of the consequent inclosure, is more than many are willing to incur. That the improvers of land should be subject to this expence is not just, and that men should be obliged to inclose these lands is neither just nor wise; because hedge-rows consume much land, stint the growth of corn, cause it to lodge, prevent its drying, and harbour birds. If men are left at liberty, without restraint, when they find it for their interest to inclose, they will inclose.

Should the House of Commons, agreeable to the resolutions of 1775, enter seriously into this business, and adopt such regulations as may effectually relieve the public from the grievous and still increasing burthen, which for more than half a century has been the subject of serious investigation and of loud complaints; it will be necessary for magistrates to pay more than common attention to the police, till industry and subordination shall be once more restored. The reins have been held with a loose hand, at a time when the idleness and extravagance, the drunkenness and dissipation, with the consequent crimes and vices of the lower classes of the people, called for the most strenuous exertions of the magistrate, and the most strict execution of the laws.

If the labouring poor, in health, previous to marriage, and whilst their families are small, are compelled to raise a fund for their own support, in case of sickness or old age; there can be no doubt, that when at any time, from peculiar circumstances, this fund shall prove inadequate, the most liberal contributions will be made to relieve any occasional distress. No one can doubt of this, who has witnessed the generous efforts which were lately made to assist the woollen manufacturers in Gloucestershire during the stagnation of their trade. Money was collected for them from all the adjacent counties, and in the metropolis, to feed and to employ them. At Minchin Hampton in particular, when the poor's tax was seven shillings in the pound on the rack rents, and their poor were more than commonly distressed, two thousand two hundred persons were cloathed, fed, and set to work, by voluntary benefactions. It should be added, for the credit of these poor people, that they worked from six in the morning till eight at night. Had the manufacture fallen to rise no more, the manufacturers must in reason have retired, or must have turned their hands to something else; because no fund, no tax, no charitable contributions, can support such a multitude of people when their trade is gone. In cases of sudden emergency assistance will be loudly called for, and the affluent will not be tardy in sending a supply. The English have never yet been charged with want of charity. They need not many arguments to excite their pity and compassion: the only difficulty is to restrain the impetuosity of their benevolence, and to direct their bounty towards the most worthy objects.

Besides these sudden emergencies, affecting the whole districts where extensive manufactures are established, individuals must be ever subject to occasional distress, from various accidents and from unexpected losses, which, without the kind assistance of a friend, they are not able to support. In such circumstances, where can the sufferer look for help? Not to the overseers of the poor; for their authority does not extend beyond food and raiment. To make good his losses, and to support him in his station, industry in distress can find no sufficient refuge but in the generous aid of his more affluent and charitable neighbours. This refuge will never fail him; nor will they ever suffer him to want, if they are able to relieve him, and if he has proved himself worthy of compassion.

To relieve the poor by voluntary donations is not only most wise, politic, and just; is not only most agreeable both to reason and to revelation; but it is most effectual in preventing misery, and most excellent in itself, as cherishing, instead of rancour, malice, and contention, the opposite and most amiable affections of the human breast, pity, compassion, and benevolence in the rich, love, reverence, and gratitude in the poor. Nothing in nature can be more disgusting than a parish pay-table, attendant upon which, in the same objects of misery, are too often found combined, snuff, gin, rags, vermin, insolence, and abusive language; nor in nature can any thing be more beautiful than the mild complacency of benevolence, hastening to the humble cottage to relieve the wants of industry and virtue, to feed the hungry, to cloath the naked, and to sooth the sorrows of the widow with her tender orphans; nothing can be more pleasing, unless it be their sparkling eyes, their bursting tears, and their uplifted hands, the artless expressions of unfeigned gratitude for unexpected favours. Such scenes will frequently occur whenever man shall have power to dispose of their own property. When the poor are obliged to cultivate the friendship of the rich, the rich will never want inclination to relieve the distresses of the poor.

FINIS.

AFTERWORD

JOSEPH Townsend's concern for the character and effect of the Poor Law was no more abiding than that of multitudes of eighteenth and early nineteenth-century Englishmen, although it may have been more forcefully enunciated. The preoccupation of Townsend's contemporaries with that code is not surprising. The Poor Law intruded into the lives and pocketbooks of ordinary men more directly and persistently than did any other instrument of government. By far the greater part of the sums that the subject paid for the security and maintenance of his kingdom normally went to the relief of its poor. Although national statistics pertaining to the number of persons on relief at any one time are unreliable for this period, it is certainly true that many Englishmen, particularly in years of shortages and high prices, could find a third or even more of their neighbors wholly or in part dependent on the support the Poor Law provided. In brief, the Poor Law and its implementation were a major component of life in Joseph Townsend's England, and no understanding of the author or his nation is possible without an appreciation of this fact.

I

UNTIL 1834 and the "New Poor Law" of that year, English law concerning the relief of the poor was based upon a series of Elizabethan statutes, most notably the act of

1597/1598 (39 Elizabeth c. 3). This measure, itself partly a refinement of earlier statutes, ordered the appointment of overseers of the poor in every parish, who were empowered "to raise weekly or otherwise by taxation of every inhabitant, and every occupier of lands in the said parish, in such competent sum and sums of money as they shall think fit; a convenient stock of flax, hemp, wool, thread, iron and other necessary ware and stuff to set the poor on work; and also competent sums of money for and towards the necessary relief of the lame, impotent, old, blind, and such other among them being poor and not able to work." The appointment of overseers (except in the case of parish church-wardens, who were overseers *ex officio*) was the responsibility of two justices of the peace, to whom the overseers were to render their accounts annually. The principle of parish responsibility for the impotent and able-bodied poor under the supervision of the magistrates was confirmed in 1601 (43 Elizabeth c. 2) and remained the foundation of the English Poor Law for nearly two and a half centuries.

Although they specified that a stock of materials be supplied by every parish, upon which the able-bodied poor would labor, neither of the great Elizabethan statutes specified the creation of buildings in which this work might be carried on. In the reign of James I (7 James I c. 4, 1609/1610) an effort was made in that direction; houses of correction were now required in every county, where work would be provided for both the disorderly and simply destitute persons maintained there. It is uncertain how often the houses of correction ultimately established under this act were chiefly places of work for innocent able-bodied poor, or penal institutions for the troublesome. But in time the idea of a workhouse as a place in which laboring paupers might be both provided for, and compelled to work so efficiently that the institution would show a profit, became a popular one. By the

last years of the seventeenth century many unions of
urban parishes were being created by private acts of Parliament for the purpose of erecting common workhouses
in which inmates would be kept in an orderly state while
increasing, in their own small way, the wealth of the nation. These "corporations of the poor," the most well-
known of which was established at Bristol in 1696, never
returned the profits expected of them, but they did provide the model for an important public act in 1723 (9
George I c. 7). This statute empowered parish officers to
purchase or hire, with the vestry's consent, a workhouse
into which all the poor of the parish, including the infant,
aged and infirm as well as the able-bodied, might be forci-
bly removed. If any pauper refused to leave his home for
the dubious comforts of the workhouse, he was hence-
forth to be denied relief. Parishes too small to provide
their own workhouse establishments could unite for the
purpose. The act of 1723 was widely adopted because it
appeared to offer the overseers a "workhouse test" which
would discourage many paupers from seeking relief, and
people who agreed to accept maintenance under those
terms would be likely to cost the parish less than if they
were receiving "out-relief" in their own homes.

Out-relief payments continued in many places, however. Indeed, since the general disappearance by 1650 of
those parish stocks specified in the Elizabethan statutes,
precincts that did not build adequate workhouses had no
choice but to relieve their paupers, even able-bodied ones,
by way of regular or occasional doles. In 1782 the principle
of out-relief to the able-bodied received legislative sanction with a measure (22 George III c. 83) often referred
to as Gilbert's Act after its sponsor Thomas Gilbert,
M.P. for Lichfield. According to this act, which a parish
could adopt with the consent of two-thirds of its ratepayers, a salaried "guardian of the poor" would be nomi-
nated by the parish to perform many functions previously

the responsibility of unpaid and often negligent overseers. The new officers were enabled, under the magistrates' supervision, to establish and maintain workhouses within their individual parishes or unions of parishes. However, unlike the workhouses created pursuant to the statute of 1723, these Gilbert Act institutions were intended only for the occupancy of orphaned and dependent children and "such as are become indigent by old age, sickness, or infirmities, and are unable to acquire a maintenance by their labour." Able-bodied paupers were to be found employment by the parish guardians or, if work could not be procured, they were to be maintained by out-relief. Too, the guardians were required to make up wages of employed persons whose incomes were inadequate for their support. Gilbert's Act was not widely adopted, but its passage probably further encouraged the practice of allowances-in-aid-of-wages and other sorts of money payments to able-bodied paupers. In 1796 (36 George III c. 23) that part of the 1723 act which prohibited relief being given the poor in their own homes was repealed, and now every parish overseer, with the consent of the vestry, could provide out-relief to any able-bodied or other pauper without first applying the workhouse test.

During the last twenty years of the Old Poor Law, from the end of the Napoleonic Wars in 1815 until the adoption of the Poor Law Amendment Act of 1834, many political and literary energies were expended on the question of the responsibility of society for its less fortunate members. However, during these two decades actual legislative accomplishments relating to poor relief were not impressive. In 1819 a statute of some importance (59 George III c. 22) permitted parishes to elect committees called "select vestries" for the management of all matters pertaining to the poor, and to appoint salaried "assistant overseers" in place of the traditional unpaid officers. The chief intention of the measure was to encourage a greater concern and efficiency in the treatment of poverty on the local level, and the act, which was adopted in many places, did at first seem responsible for stricter management and diminished poor rates. But the same failings of parochial apathy and jobbery which had typified many old "open" vestries came to afflict the select vestries as well, and by the early 1830s it was widely recognized that this expedient had failed and that more sweeping reform was called for. The Poor Law Amendment Act (4 and 5 William IV c. 76), following the monumental research of the Poor Law Inquiry Commissioners, was the result. The framers of this vastly important (many would say tragic) statute reached back across the years to the workhouse test principle of 1723 and combined virtually all of the parishes in England into large workhouse unions governed by locally elected "boards of guardians." The entire mechanism was made the responsibility of poor-law commissioners appointed by the government, the "three Bashaws of Somerset House." Whatever else the New Poor Law accomplished (there is much disagreement on the character of its accomplishments), it meant the end of the parish as the chief local unit of statutory relief, and the end of the magistrate as supervisor of local practice. It meant, in brief, the end of the Old Poor Law—and the ascension of a social philosophy and regime whose echoes persisted until the National Assistance Act of 1948.

Accompanying the Old Poor Law for most of its career was a body of enactments known collectively as the Law of Settlement and Removal. The genesis of this law may be found in an act of 1662 (13 and 14 Charles II c. 12). Here it was declared that a stranger coming into a parish who did not thereupon rent a property with a £10 annual rental, or otherwise give evidence of financial independence, might, on the complaint of the parish officers and by the warrant of two justices, be removed back to the parish where he had been originally settled "as a native householder, sojourner, apprentice, or servant." An exception was made for temporary residents like harvesters; they were not removable providing they brought certificates from their own parishes acknowledging they had "settlements" there entitling them to relief. Finally, the act promised stern punishment for anyone who, having once been returned to his own parish, made his way back to the place from which he had been removed.

For half a century various statutes augmented the act of 1662, chiefly in the way of making legal settlements more difficult to obtain. In spite of angry complaints from a growing host of commentators (Adam Smith and Joseph Townsend among them) that the Law of Settlement and Removal prompted wasteful expenditure on removals and attendant litigation and drastically inhibited the labor traffic, it was not until 1795 (35 George III c. 101) that the first step was taken to meliorate the effects of the law; removal of persons to their own parishes was prohibited until they actually became paupers and sought parish relief. The principle of removability proved to be tenacious, however. In one form or another it clung to life, disappearing only with the Poor Law itself in 1948.

There was another corpus of law relating to the management of the poor which ought to be briefly mentioned. This pertained to vagrants, and like the central body of the Poor Law it owed most of its character to legislation of Elizabeth's time. An act of 1597/1598 (39 Elizabeth c. 4) provided for the apprehension and punishment of "rogues, vagabonds, or sturdy beggars" who were found begging, wandering, or behaving in a disorderly fashion. Upon the order of a single justice any man or woman answering this description was to be stripped to the waist and whipped "until his or her body be bloody." The vagrant was then to be passed to his parish of birth or last residence or, if he seemed incorrigible, confined to prison until the next quarter sessions, when the magistrates might order him banished from the realm. During the following two centuries this act was amended and altered perhaps fifty times. In 1744 an important recodification (17 George II c. 5) delineated more specifically the various classes of offenders and punishments. Finally in 1822 (3 George IV c. 40) most sorts of vagrants were no longer to be automatically removed to their parishes of settlement, as had been done previously. Instead, they were to be treated like any other criminals, liable to sentences of imprisonment at hard labor. Henceforward only when he applied for relief was the vagrant to be sent to his parish of settlement, and now he appeared in the character of an ordinary pauper, subject to the ubiquitous Law of Settlement and Removal.

II

FOR all the importance of the statutory Poor Law, understanding of the practical operation of poor relief and management before 1834 lies largely in the knowledge— or at least awareness—of local practice. In the first place, many acts pertaining to the poor in those years were only an extension and ratification of parochial and other local developments. Many municipal corporations and county quarter sessions had established houses of correction, partly for the purpose of setting the innocent poor to work, long before the statute of 1607 legitimized this device. Prior to the Act of Settlement of 1662 uncounted numbers of parishes were refusing to admit strangers who appeared to have insufficient resources. Certainly the widespread distribution of out-relief to all classes of paupers in the wake of the grain scarcity of 1795, memorialized by the Berkshire magistrates' famous "Speenham-land" table of allowances, largely inspired the 1796 statute which sanctioned this practice. Select vestries and salaried assistant overseers were not altogether new with the statute of 1819, and the device of the "labour rate," intended to provide more general employment for the poor without unduly burdening the parish ratepayers, was not regularized until 1832 (2 and 3 William IV c. 96).

A corollary to this characteristic of Poor Law administration is that local authorities, including justices of the peace and officials of the fifteen thousand English and Welsh parishes under their supervision, often went their own way on questions of poor relief, irrespective of Parliament's commands. Magistrates frequently neglected the clause of the 1597/1598 statute which demanded they inspect the accounts of out-going overseers, and the overseers didn't trouble to remind them of it. The justices seldom inflicted the harsh punishments the Act of Settlement called down upon those who returned to the parishes from which they had been removed. A major impediment to effective vagrancy laws was the unwillingness of magistrates to enforce the cruel whipping clauses; vagrants were simply passed back to their own parishes from which they might stray again, untroubled by the prospect of bloodied backs. In 1697 Parliament passed an unusual measure (8 and 9 William III c. 30). In future all persons receiving parish relief were to "openly wear upon the shoulder of the right sleeve a badge or mark with a large Roman P, and the first letter of the name of the parish . . . in red or blue cloth." Even in the years directly after its passage this act was not universally heeded, and by the time the law was repealed in 1810 it was an unusual parish vestry indeed that demanded paupers be thus branded. It has already been noted that by the middle of the seventeenth century the parish stocks specified in the Elizabethan statutes were no longer collected, and how for a century and a half, in place of this provision, great numbers of parishes supported their able-bodied poor by way of entirely extralegal doles. In the years after 1796, when this sort of relief had legislative approval, many parishes continued to exhibit their traditional autonomy, now in reference to the magistrates' attempts to compel the use of countywide, Speenhamland-like tables of allowances. It might be added that the persistent disaffection of the parishes for higher authority would have been still more visible had not important Poor Law legislation of the eighteenth and early nineteenth centuries been "adoptive" in character; that is, subject in every locality to the endorsement of the parish vestry.

Here the interested observer might ask: if England consisted of fifteen thousand sometimes-sovereign states so far as Poor Law administration was concerned, how can one possibly hope to isolate general characteristics, trends, or attitudes pertaining to this administration, short of laying bare the particulars of poor relief and management in every one of those places, across perhaps two hundred and fifty years? He might be all the more discouraged, realizing that parish overseers, with whom the chief responsibility for local administration lay, were annual appointments. Thus, even in the single parish, the least continuity of characteristics would seem unlikely.

In fact, parish studies undertaken so far indicate that certain basic, ascertainable, socioeconomic and demographic factors helped shape the local character of poverty and its relief. In the first place, although every parish overseer left his own mark on his year's administration, overseers in both urban and rural parishes almost always came from those classes who most directly paid the poor rates, normally pertaining to occupiers rather than absentee owners. Accordingly parish administrations usually tended to a certain practicality; specific remedies were adopted for particular difficulties. There was relatively little concern for the latest fashions in poor relief dogma beyond quickened interest in cost-saving devices when poor rates were oppressive. Further, those difficulties were often of a different kind among populous urban parishes than among small rural ones, and so also were responses to them. The crowded neighborhoods of London, for example, were plagued by beggars and vagrants to a degree foreign to most other places. The overtaxed machinery of justice could not control these multitudes, and here magistrates and parish officers, resigned to the circumstances, were most likely to neglect the vagrancy laws altogether. The coming of manufactures to once agricultural areas brought new problems for parish officers and resources. Unexpected depression in the local industry might engender unemployment and poverty on such a scale that they could not be handled within the traditional framework of relief.

In still rural countryside the specific economy dictated much of the character of poverty and relief. Communities where livestock and dairy farming dominated were normally less troubled by severe seasonal unemployment than was the case in grain-producing regions, where an economy that demanded legions of hands at harvest time simply came full stop, except for threshing, during the winter months. Not surprisingly it was among the counties of southern and eastern England, where cereal production reigned, that the giving of out-relief to the able-bodied poor became widespread, especially during the dead part of the agricultural year.

Of course it is true that no amount of investigation into the social and economic conditions of a parish can promise complete understanding of poor-relief practices in that neighborhood; the unpredictable and idiosyncratic play their troublesome parts. Nevertheless, it is a fact that poor relief must not be studied *in vacuo*. It pertains intimately to the greater socioeconomic whole, and its operation cannot be intelligently perceived unless the entire spectrum of associated matters is kept in view.

III

THE Old Poor Law is an astonishingly rich source for illuminating a portion of England's past. Documents shedding light on parochial practice, and the deliberations of magistrates in quarter and lesser sessions, lie heaped to the ceilings of county record offices, waiting the historian's attention. These materials, together with evidence from parliamentary papers, Home Office Records, and from the statutes themselves, have brought, and will continue to bring, a more abundant knowledge and appreciation of relations in these centuries between the various levels of authority, and between all government and the society it was supposed to rule and care for.

Today a growing community of scholars is addressing itself to the operation of the Old Poor Law as a key to understanding questions of specific and general significance. Professor Mark Blaug has recently likened English circumstances soon after the turn of the nineteenth century to those of an underdeveloped country anywhere, and his conclusions regarding the utility of out-relief at that time have wider application than the English experience only. More recently still, James P. Huzel at the University of Kent has contributed his opinion to the discussion of whether the Old Poor Law in those years, by providing a basic subsistence for even the most pauperized, measurably encouraged population growth in England. (He believes it did not.) Other investigators have turned more exclusively to parish records, testing old assumptions and assessments (the universal application of "Speenhamland" tables, for example) against the most local and detailed of document collections. For these historians, and for all who are concerned with the history of social attitudes and welfare, the republication of Joseph Townsend's remarkable *Dissertation on the Poor Laws* is an overdue, and most welcome, event.

Bucknell University   MARK NEUMAN

BIBLIOGRAPHICAL NOTE
ON THE OLD POOR LAW

EVERY student of the Old Poor Law must begin with the classic investigations of the subject by Sidney and Beatrice Webb, contained in *The Parish and the County* (London: Longmans, Green, 1906) and *English Poor Law History: Part I; The Old Poor Law* and *Part II; The Last Hundred Years*, vol. 1 (London: Longmans, Green, 1927 and 1929). For particulars of every statute relating to the Poor Law before 1834 the historian may wish to refer to Sir George Nicholls's two volume *History of the English Poor Law* (London: John Murray, 1854). The dismaying intricacies of the system of poor rates under the Old Poor Law are unravelled in Edwin Cannan's *The History of Local Rates in England* (London: P. S. King and Son, 1927).

In her very readable *The English Poor in the Eighteenth Century* (London: George Routledge and Sons, 1926), Dorothy Marshall points out how great the distance was in that time between the admirable theory and unsuccessful practice of the Poor Law. She attributes the failures of the system chiefly to the inadequate financial and intellectual resources of parish administrations. J. D. Marshall's brief essay "The Old Poor Law 1795–1834" in *Studies in Economic History*, ed. M. W. Flinn (London: Macmillan, 1968) is a review of recent arguments pertaining to the singular developments in poor-relief practices during those years. *The Early History of English Poor Relief* by E. M. Leonard (Cambridge: Cambridge University Press, 1900) is an assessment of the management of the poor before 1650. It is dated but nonetheless useful for reference. Thomas Garden Barnes's *Somerset 1625–1640: A County's Government During the "Personal Rule"* (Cambridge, Mass.: Harvard University Press, 1961) is a closely reasoned study of the impact of the reign of Charles I upon the activities and loyalties of the Somerset magistracy.

The "Book of Orders," with its directions for the forceful implementation of the Poor Law, occupies much of the author's attention, and his discussion of the administration of poor relief indicates how out-of-date Leonard's earlier study has in fact become. An interesting investigation of the changing character of a county bench in a later time is Peter Styles's "The Development of County Administration in the Late XVIIIth and Early XIXth Centuries, *Dugdale Society Occasional Papers* 4 (1934). Styles's subject is the Warwickshire magistracy, but his conclusions about those local governors, who were charged with supervising the operation of the Poor Law, probably have a wider application.

Mark Blaug's opinions on the character and effect of allowances to the able-bodied under the Old Poor Law are found in two recent articles, "The Myth of the Old Poor Law and the Making of the New," *Journal of Economic History* 23 (1963): 151–184, and "The Poor Law Report Reexamined," *Journal of Economic History* 24 (1964): 229–245. James P. Huzel's "Malthus, the Poor Law, and Population in Early Nineteenth Century England," *Economic History Review* 2d ser. 22 (1969): 430–452, includes that scholar's thoughts on the possible association of relief levels and population growth. In their passionately argued *The Village Labourer 1760–1832* (London: Longmans, Green, 1913), J. L. and Barbara Hammond insist that "Speenhamland" allowances were largely responsible for the tragic deterioration of the rural laborer's condition during that time. In *The Great Transformation: The Political and Economic Origins of Our Time* (New York: Farrar and Rinehart, 1944) Karl Polanyi credits "Speenhamland" with preventing working people from coping successfully with the early effects of the modern market economy. Arthur Redford's *Labour Migration in England 1800–1850*, 2d ed. rev. (Manchester: Manchester University Press, 1964) argues that indiscriminate allowances under the Old Poor Law inhibited the movement of labor to the newly industrialized parts of England far more than did the Laws of Settlement and Removal. The developing precepts of humanity which encouraged a more generous attitude toward the poor in the last quarter of the eighteenth century, and ensured support for Gilbert's Act and out-relief to the able-bodied, are intelligently discussed in A. W. Coats's "Economic Thought and Poor Law Policy in the Eighteenth Century," *Economic History Review* 2d ser. 13 (1960): 39–51.

Many commentators on the Old Poor Law emphasize the debt that legislation frequently owed to the example of local practice, whereas others denounce the notion that, once enacted, statutory commands entirely overrode local custom. Dorothy Marshall focuses on local variations in poor relief practice in both *The English Poor in the Eighteenth Century* (see above) and "The Old Poor Law, 1662–1795," *Economic History Review* 8 (1937): 38–47. Philip Styles's "The Evolution of the Law of Settlement," *University of Birmingham Historical Journal* 9 (1963/64): 33–63, and J. D. Marshall's "The Nottinghamshire Reformers and their Contribution to the New Poor Law," *Economic History Review* 2d ser. 13 (1961): 382–396, trace the effects of local precedents upon crucial Poor Law enactments.

Joseph Townsend's *Dissertation on the Poor Laws* is visible evidence of a large and growing demand for the reform, and even abolition, of the laws then governing poor relief. The ebb and flow of opinions on the character of present and proposed Poor Laws in the decades prior to the Poor Law Amendment Act are delineated in J. R. Poynter's *Society and Pauperism: English Ideas on Poor Relief, 1795–1834* (London: Routledge and Kegan Paul, 1969), and Judith B. Williams's annotated *Guide to the Printed Materials for English Social and Economic History*, 2 vols. (New York: Columbia University Press, 1926) catalogues all of the extensive literature which grew around questions of Poor Law theory and practice after the middle of the eighteenth century.

The following titles are a selection from the many thoughtful and informative later studies which pertain, wholly or in part, to the administration of the Old Poor Law in particular localities.

Ashby, A. W. *One Hundred Years of Poor Law Administration in a Warwickshire Village.* Oxford Studies in Social and Legal History, edited by Paul Vinogradoff. Oxford: Clarendon Press, 1912.

Emmison, F. G. "The Relief of the Poor in Eaton Socon, 1706–1834." *Bedfordshire Historical Record Society* 15 (1933): 1–98.

Goodman, P. H. "Eighteenth Century Poor Law Administration in the Parish of Oswestry." *Transactions of the Shropshire Archaeological Society* 56 (1960): 328–342.

Hampson, E. M. *The Treatment of Poverty in Cambridgeshire, 1597–1834.* Cambridge: Cambridge University Press, 1934.

Mitchelson, N. "The Old Poor Law in East Yorkshire." *East Yorkshire Local History Series* 2 (1953).

Sheppard, F. H. W. *Local Government in St. Marylebone 1688–1835.* London: Athlone Press, 1958.

Taylor, J. S. "Poverty in a West Devon Parish (Bradford) in the last years of the Old Poor Law." *Transactions of the Devonshire Association* 101 (1969): 161–182.

Most authors of local histories of the Old Poor Law depend for their evidence chiefly upon parish accounts and papers, the great bulk of which are now deposited in county record offices. Some idea of what those parish documents contain may be found in W. E. Tate's *The Parish Chest* (Cambridge: Cambridge University Press, 1946), and in the growing list of published document collections issuing from county and other historical societies. In *Archives and Local History* (London: Methuen, 1966), F. G. Emmison describes additional kinds of pertinent records likely to be discovered in a county record office. A convenient, if selective, guide to parliamentary reports, returns, and other papers dealing with poverty and its relief is *Hansard's Catalogue and Breviate of Parliamentary Papers 1696–1834,* edited by P. and G. Ford (Oxford: Basil Blackwell, 1953).